MEN AND LETTERS

MEN AND LETTERS

ESSAYS IN CHARACTERIZATION
AND CRITICISM

BY

HORACE E. SCUDDER

Essay Index Reprint Series

 BOOKS FOR LIBRARIES PRESS
FREEPORT, NEW YORK

First Published 1887
Reprinted 1972

PS
121
S 3
1972

Library of Congress Cataloging in Publication Data

Scudder, Horace Elisha, 1838-1902.
    Men and letters.

    (Essay index reprint series)
    Reprint of the 1887 ed.
    CONTENTS: Elisha Mulford.--Longfellow and his art.
--A modern prophet. [etc.]
    1. English literature--Addresses, essays, lectures
2. American literature--Addresses, essays, lectures.
I. Title.
PS121.S3 1972   810.9   75-37528
ISBN 0-8369-2569-6

PRINTED IN THE UNITED STATES OF AMERICA
BY
NEW WORLD BOOK MANUFACTURING CO., INC.
HALLANDALE, FLORIDA 33009

To

HENRY MILLS ALDEN,

DOCTOR OF LETTERS.

My dear Alden, —

In that former state of existence when we were poets, you wrote verses which I knew by heart and I read dreamy tales to you which you speculated over as if they were already classics. Then you bound your manuscript verses in a full blue calf volume and put it on the shelf, and I woke to find myself at the desk of a literary workman. We used to be told that seven years was the limit of personal integrity, but I believe the physiologists now refuse to let us be the same person for two consecutive breaths. Nearly four sevens of years have passed since we had daily and nightly companionship, and perhaps we ought to feel some hesitation in identifying ourselves with the

two young poets who walked Broadway and
haunted little back rooms in Fourth Avenue
and Eleventh Street; who had theories
about Homer and discussed them in Har-
lem ; who spent money before it was earned,
and proposed the prudent course of retiring
altogether upon an unexpected windfall of
a hundred dollars, using the leisure thus
happily secured for executing the epical
work which required a continuity of time
not easily had under customary conditions.

It would be hard indeed if we were forced
to tie those days to these by the brief notes
and rare visits which have carelessly happened between us. Let me rather think
that Memory plays her part graciously and
helps each to a proper sense of the other's
past, when Consciousness takes a nap and
refuses to respond readily to our call. I
wonder if you are as reluctant to open that
blue calf book as I to re-read certain early
fancies of mine? Yet I am credulous
enough to think that the verses you wrote
have re-sung themselves in that sympathetic,

patient, discriminating life which you have led as a literary judge, for I find myself curiously susceptible in my own work to certain influences which once shaped my thought into more creative form.

Be this as it may, the friendliness which led you to listen to me when I had scarcely any other audience gives me some courage to come out from behind the screen of anonymity which has permitted me to work with freedom the past dozen years. At least I shall have one generous friend who will read what I have written because I wrote it, and that, I suppose, is the meaning of the personal equation of which philosophers talk so sagely. Criticism, when anonymous, is still personal ; the critic is a person. But when he signs his name he introduces the other person, his double, himself reflected in the mind of his reader. My occupation has compelled me to print much comment upon contemporaneous literature ; fortunately, I have been able for the most part to work out of the glare of publicity. But there is always that something in us which whispers *I*, and after a while the anonymous critic becomes a little tired of listening to the whisper in his solitary cave, and is disposed to escape from it by coming out into the light even at the risk of blinking a little, and by suffering the ghostly voice to become articulate, though the sound startle him. One craves company for his thought, and is not quite content always to sit in the dark with his guests.

Accept then this little book, my dear Alden, and be my one reader, — surely that is the least return one can make for having a book dedicated to him, — and thus recover with me something of the illusion of days which were no better than these, not so good as they, we may each well think, but still days when the sun rose a little earlier and set a little later.

Faithfully yours,
H. E. SCUDDER.

CAMBRIDGE, MASS.,
    1 *October*, 1887.

CONTENTS.

MEN AND LETTERS.

———◆———

ELISHA MULFORD.

IT is a pity that some painter of insight and with skill of interpretation had not given us a portrait of Elisha Mulford, when he was in his full strength. It is an idle wish that art might find some means of perpetuating for us that most delicate organ of personality, the human voice. The painter, if he be given the precious power of seeing, can repair the waste of memory, and long after eyes have closed in death their power of appeal may dwell in some counterfeit presentment of art; but the lips have no language, and what musician has yet been able to recover for us the sound of a voice that is still? There is not a more lasting note of recognition between persons than the voice, which betrays the forgotten friend when the eye scans the face in vain for any trace of remembered lineaments. It is the last, finest expression of the person, the most impossible

to evade or simulate, the absolutely uncon-
veyable.   It was the misery of the poor old
blind Isaac that he allowed himself to trust
his sense of touch rather than his more unerring sense of hearing.

There are some natures that reveal themselves with peculiar clearness through the
voice, and Mulford was one of these. I cannot take up his books or one of his friendly
letters without hearing that singularly rhythmical, harmonious utterance.   In the pulpit,
where he was rarely heard of late years, it
fell into a somewhat monotonous series of
cadences, due, very likely, to the physical
exertion of a speaker who suffered from de-
fective hearing ; but in conversation, his
voice, low and even, swung in periods which
were full of an incommunicable beauty.
When he read aloud some favorite passage,
one seemed to be listening to a sort of holy
chant, and there are passages in *The Republic of God* which sound in the ear like felicitous renderings of some ancient Latin hymn
of the church.   It chanced to me to read
this book on shipboard, and I found myself
reading page after page in apparently perfect agreement with the great metronome of
the deep sea swell.

It is the rarity of Mulford's nature, finding an outlet in his voice and radiating from his person, which immediately addresses one who attempts to record impressions of a man of such singular fascination. The reason for this personal power lay deep. Back of voice and personal presence, one felt the existence of a remarkable harmony of life. Mulford never seemed to require any adjustment of himself. That profound consciousness of enduring relations which lies at the core of his writings was not a philosophic attainment with him, but an endowment of nature, and it exhibited itself in trivial circumstances. I suspect that deafness was something of a reinforcement to a temperament like his. He heard everything that he needed to hear, but was conveniently rid of a multitude of distracting or discordant sounds; and so he kept on his way, a curious spectator of life, wonderfully interested in all the details of politics, of business, and of literature, yet somehow making all these details subservient to certain great currents of thought upon which his mind was always sailing.

This largeness of nature disclosed itself in his habitual treatment of philosophical or

political questions. A man of science would
say that he had a scientific mind, which was
capable of considering a subject, no matter
what might be its personal bearings, in an
abstracted, impersonal light; and I have
heard such a man express his surprise that
one with a theological training could so ap-
proach subjects which involved theological
positions. It was this freedom from polemic
considerations which made his discourse on
all themes agreeable. He did not like a dis-
pute; he had no disposition to drag his wits
into any boxing - match with other people's
wits; and thus he was often silent and apparently in polite conformity with his neighbor,
when his real thought was quite remote. Indeed, he carried this so far that he sometimes
felt his way with his friends, and waited to
be assured of their general agreement before
he would give them his thought.

He was not a reformer and he was not a
partisan. There was a singular fault of timidity in his nature, due in part to the isola-
tion in which he dwelt; but it was only a
fault, for he was fearless in his thought,
and when he knew with whom he was talking and that he would not be misunderstood,
he was unreserved in the expression of his

thought. He suffered in some men's judgment for this, I think, for there are always
those who are impatient if the men on their
side, as they say, do not come out squarely.
Mulford had the patience of a scholar, and
the sense of large relations which made him
hesitate about taking a position which would
identify him with some particular party or
sect. I am doing him no injustice when I
say that he struck out in the proofs the passage from his book, *The Nation*, which carried his statement regarding the ballot to its
logical conclusion in woman suffrage. He
did not retract his personal opinion, and he
left all the premises for the advocates of woman suffrage to use, but he did not mean to
identify himself with a special propaganda.
He knew that if he did, many persons would
read his book as if it had only that sentence
in it, and he refused to have his larger
thought turned into a shibboleth. It was
this comprehensiveness of his mind which
dwarfed many of the petty distinctions to
which others clung, and made him sought
by men of the most contradictory views.
More than this, his comprehensiveness was
not mere tolerance, and it was impossible to
give him a name which implied a philosophic

eclecticism. Others might for convenience dub him a Broad Churchman in theology, but a High Churchman would have found him in many respects congenial and might zealously have claimed him. It is only party men who are uneasy unless they can label other persons. Mulford never labelled his associates, and no one who obtained a real insight of his nature felt any disposition to label him.

Under the simple condition of general sympathy, his gift of thought was most generous. He published but two books and a few magazine or newspaper articles, and he delivered but one or two courses of lectures in theology. Yet he gave not merely to his friends, he lavished upon any appreciative listener, with unstinting freedom, the product of his thought on a wide range of subjects. If any one has kept a record of Mulford's monologues, and has faithfully reported his speech, he ought to give it to the public. I call them monologues, for brief-ness' sake, but there was in Mulford's talk none of that vain love of intellectual display which is apt to affect monologue. It was a pleasure to him to talk, but he liked to take the cue from his friend. His deafness stood somewhat in the way of free conversation, but there must have been few of his friends who would not rather listen than do more than just keep him supplied with topics. Indeed, he had a little trick of which he seemed only partially aware. If very much absorbed in what he was saying, he would idly push his ear-trumpet almost out of reach; it was a signal to his neighbor not to interrupt him. Then, when he had had his say, he would secure the trumpet again, hold it up, and intimate his readiness to hear what was to be said to that. Shut out largely from general intercourse with people, he made much of his friends in the way of familiar visits. At the end of an evening, when one was laying aside books and papers, a ring at the bell would announce a caller. Enter Mulford, very doubtful about putting aside his hat and coat: he had come in merely for a moment; he could not stay. Then one put more wood on the fire, and settled one's self to that three or four hours' talk which was sure to follow, with good-byes at last under the stars at midnight, that seemed nearer than before.

The miracle which he worked in his conversation with friends was the multiplication of their thoughts. One brought to him one's latest idea or scheme, — it was always easy to do that, — and Mulford took it, reflected a moment, and gave it back enlarged, enriched, set in wide relations, and illuminated by a sudden glory. That positiveness which rules in his writings was a delightful quality in his personal judgments. He spoke as one having authority, not as a special pleader; for the results which he announced were reached not by a careful weighing of evidence, but by a clear, direct perception which went at once to the bottom of the matter. There was a deliberation in his manner which added weight to what he said, and gave a convincing tone which seemed at the time to go further than an argument. A friend who was about to deliver a course of lectures allowed himself to speak with misgivings of his undertaking. Mulford thought a moment, turned aside his head in his sage way, and presently declared himself somewhat as follows : —

" Now, there is no one within sight or sound of Boston who knows as much upon this subject as you do. Therefore you should give your lectures without fear or favor. You have no apology to make. You must speak with authority."

He evidently thought his friend needed a little bracing, but his manner of reinforcing him was his own. For Mulford was generous in his endowment of his friends. Many a person has acquired new confidence in himself because Mulford believed in him so thoroughly. His imagination was busy over those whom he loved. He sometimes made them over, clothing them with all the attributes they ought to have, but in such cases he wrought upon qualities which he recognized; seizing upon some lurking excellence, he amplified it until it seemed the one characteristic of the man. It was this large charity of judgment which made his estimates of men always worth listening to.

Indeed, there was something humorously enjoyable in his way of regarding persons and places that had won his affection. He was most loyal to his own. He thought Pennsylvania unquestionably the foremost State in the Union, Susquehanna County the fairest of its divisions, and the district which took in Montrose and Friendsville the heart of the county. Then his friends in their several professions were incontestably in the front ranks, and their opinions on various subjects were well worth attention. He did not make swans of geese, by any means, but his swans were all of the best strain. There was a glamour, which never suggested the slightest insincerity, in all his regard for the men who attracted him. He was sturdily theirs, and it did one good to find so honest a lover of men.

It is also true that his friends showed themselves at their best to him. Possibly, again, his deafness helped them. It was such an effort to speak to him at any length that it was hardly worth while to give him anything but one's best thought. But this was not all. He was so eager to hear and was beforehand so sure one had something worth telling, that he quickened the wits of his friends. Besides, like begets like, and Mulford, with his generous way of looking at things, made one wish to think like him ; not necessarily with the same conclusions, but with the same breadth and comprehensiveness. Those who were most with him fell into his little mannerisms ; they caught themselves using his favorite expressions ; they had an odd sensation of echoing his style of thought. His correspondents were apt to feel his presence when they wrote to him, and to give a turn to their sentences which made them sound like Mulford's own.

He had a half-humorous fondness for his own phrases. Those sounding forms which make *The Nation* a puzzle to some readers, a revelation to others, were very apt to recur in his conversation, and to afford stepping-stones when one was crossing some stream of his thought. I remember how greatly he was pleased as well as amused by a tribute once paid to him by a Union soldier, who had fought bravely through the war, and when it was all over, and he had settled down into civil life, read *The Nation*. "I did not know before why I fought!" exclaimed the enthusiastic reader. "I know now. It was because the Nation was a Moral Organism!"

No one could have believed more devoutly in the thought which underlies this book than Mulford himself. It was no pretty piece of rhetoric to him, no well-fitting theory of political life. Nothing would have disturbed him more than to hear his belief called a theory. He wrought at the conception of his work in profound silence. He was living on the broad acres of a Pennsylvania farm, remote from men, from steam, from the confusion of cities. He walked afield with his thoughts for companions, and came back to his fireside to write in labored, compact sentences the result of his pondering. For months he shunned all but the nearest companionship, wrote no letters, but read, and kindled as he read, in the newspapers of the day; for he interpreted the common news by the thought of national life over which he was brooding. In May, 1867, he wrote, with a sigh of relief from the long tension : " I have had this incessant and imperative work, of which I have just turned the last page, and it has precluded all other work or thought, and scarcely allowed rest."

To turn the last page is with most men to be through with the work, except for some slight revision, but with Mulford it meant only that the book had its thought consecutively presented. He could now look at it as a piece of literature, and see what was to be done. A year later, in May, 1868, he wrote : " I can send the whole manuscript to you before the close of the month, excepting the close of the last chapter, which I would like to keep for a few days longer." He had spent the year in putting his book in order. Six weeks later he wrote : " I cannot justify, and only regret, the entire neglect in not answering your note earlier. If I could look upon myself apart from self, I might find some cause for it in the indifference which follows the close of so long a period as these three years of almost incessant work, but I do not like this study of these 'phenomenal phases' of action. The fact is that I have been adrift and at sea with two or three of my critics. One whose judgment I hold most highly has insisted that the style and manner of my book is not equal to its substance and thought. The estimate which they have given of the latter is so high that I will not repeat it, at least in this writing, and they claim for the book an influence and a place which is very far beyond any immediate result that I should have anticipated, if I had allowed myself to think upon it. At last, if I can do so, with no infraction of my arrangements with you,[1] I have determined to re-write the whole book, as faithfully and carefully as I can, and then I shall have the satisfaction, in any result, of having given to it my utmost endeavor. The revision will affect only the style, the illus-

---

[1] I had been acting as his intermediary with the publishing house which finally issued the book.

tration and presentation of the thought of the book, and it will not materially change the size or scope of it. I shall care rather to avoid anything like the fatigue and toil of conception which I knew was apparent in my manuscript. . . . I know the work I have imposed upon myself, and I have no doubt still how much my book may gain from it, but I have been afraid that this conclusion might impair my engagements with you. With this re-writing, I could scarcely finish my work before the close of October or the early part of November, but then, and at no later day, I could place my manuscript finally in your hands."

November came and went, and December, with promises of the book in a few weeks, in a few days, and then early in January, 1869, came a letter beginning, " I write so reluctantly in my conclusion that it may be allowed me to write abruptly. The conclusion is that I am reluctant to let my manuscript pass under your eye until I have toiled yet longer on it; that I think the work of the remaining months of the winter will be all it will require, and then I shall have at least the satisfaction of having been faithful to it. The thought has not

changed, and since last spring the book has
not added a cubit to its stature, and yet I
know how necessary the toil which art has
demanded. . . . Then my friend Mr. ——,
of whose critical judgment I have the highest
regard, has offered and insisted that at the
outset I should read it to him. That requires my going to Chicago, but I have
determined to go."

It was not till the fall of 1869 that Mulford came on with his book, to be near the
press when it was being set up. The manuscript was all ready, but he wished to ask
two or three friends to go over the proofs
with him. Those who shared in this work
will remember the looks of the proof-sheets
after they finally left the author's hands;
scarcely a sentence was left unamended, and
it was almost a surprise to see the volume
finally in April, looking as innocent of error
as most printed books. Seven times, Mulford told me, had he written the book over,
and he certainly wrote it once more when he
corrected his proofs. It was an expression
of his faith in the doctrine of his book that
when it was off his hands he grudged the
delay in putting it upon the market, since
he was impressed with the conviction that

it was needed for the fall elections! That was Mulford's way of expressing also his belief in the high range of common political thinking. I never heard of *The Nation* as a campaign document, but I have read many books and political papers and speeches since that day in which I could read *The Nation* writ over again, small and large.

I have given this little history of a remarkable book because it illustrates somewhat the intellectual habit of the author. He brooded long over his thought in fundamental matters, and was extremely critical of the final form. It was ten years before he appeared with his second book, *The Republic of God*, but the underlying thought of both books had been familiar to him in its main outline long before. They were two parts of an undivided conception of human society in its divine relations, and his mind dwelt for years in a region of thought so comprehensive that his real difficulty was in limiting and formulating his expression. He had done this twice, the second time with much more ease than the first; and I am confident that, had he lived, he would have produced books with increasing rapidity, and that he would have taken

a wide range in the discussion of sociolog-
ical, literary, scientific, and psychological
questions. These books would all have
borne the same stamp; they would have
been applications to current themes of the
philosophical faith which he held. Some
one once said, " What a narrow man Mulford is ! — but then he is narrow on great
lines." I can understand how the speaker
could have said this : he had heard Mulford
talk a few times, and had noted the recur-
rence to his favorite generalizations. But
it would be by an extraordinary stretch of
meaning that one would ever think of using
the word " narrow " in connection with Mulford. He was narrow as a cañon is narrow,
when the depth apparently contracts the
sides.

What I have said may in part explain the
conviction which those had who were nearest
to him, that the man always impressed them
as greater than his books. His books suffered from the restraint of his thought, and
because their very completeness and finality
of statement conspired to shut up the thought
in them within certain definite limits. But
in the freedom of conversation these limits
were not suggested. When he first began

to lecture before his students in theology he
was embarrassed by his notes. He had
written out what he had to say, and he
read the draft with painful care, but when
he was through with it the hour was not
gone. The young men still sat attentive,
but his formal lecture was over. He was
uneasy a moment, then he repeated a phrase;
it opened the gates, the stream of talk began
to flow, his embarrassment was at an end,
and the students were delighted with the
freshness, the life, the stimulating fullness,
of his thought. It was so always. Let
him get rid of the restrictions of a hard
and fast systematic presentation, and he was
himself again. The singular part of it was
that his extemporaneous speech, his unpre-
meditated discourse, was uncommonly fine in
form. It was not that he was now vague
where before he had been precise ; he was
free where before he had been fettered. He
once asked me about a certain person, and
I said that I did not find conversation with
him a great pleasure ; that while he regarded
conversation as a fine art, he was too much
occupied with the best form of his sentences
when he was talking. "Yes," said Mulford, " it is not hay that we want in conver-

sation, but growing grass." That was the charm of his speech. It sprang freely from his mind, and one seemed to see thought growing as the grass grows.

There was one characteristic of his conversation which he shared with other good talkers, but had in a high degree of development. He could recall conversations he had had with interesting persons, and could repeat them with great vivacity. He remembered minute details in personal history, and had that liking for gossip, where it dealt with characteristic expressions of men and women worth knowing, which is so humane and so free from pettiness. Yet he had an impatience of books of gossip. Such a book, for example, as the *Journals of J. C. Young* had no charm for him, but he would read with avidity a memoir which laid bare the thought of a strong man. He used to speak of Mark Pattison's *Isaac Casaubon* as a model of what a biography should be.

He was a wide reader, but I sometimes think he read most diligently at the two ends of literature, for he was a devourer of newspapers and a constant reader of Shakespeare. His friends, who knew his tastes, kept him supplied with a great variety of public prints, and he had an instinct for the editorial article which speaks something more than the casual opinion of some hasty writer. He thought the newspapers went deeper than the pulpit in their tone during the summer of Garfield's sickness, and he listened eagerly to the roar of the great city which he heard as he scanned the columns of the city papers. And Shakespeare! He never tired of studying human thought as it was presented in the men and women of Shakespeare's drama. His fine literary sense and his insight of character found here their fullest intellectual enjoyment. He liked to read his Shakespeare in an edition which was a fac-simile of the first folio; his imagination thus brought him more directly into Shakespeare's presence. That world of life shut up within the covers of a book was a city which he visited often; he knew it by heart in the best sense, and no actor could present Shakespeare but Mulford brought to bear a criticism which was far beyond any mere judgment of fidelity to text, or even to accepted versions of character. It was a penetrating and illuminating judgment of the Shakespearean person who was under representation. The reader of *The Nation* will have

been struck by the frequent felicitous cita-
tions from Shakespeare. Mulford's regard
for Shakespeare as a political thinker was
very great, and he was constantly bearing
testimony to this effect. He regarded him
also as a great humanizer, and used to express the wish that the missionaries might
translate Shakespeare into the Chinese
tongue ; he thought the people of China
needed nothing so much.

There are some men whose speculations
are of such a nature that one feels a wistful
desire to know what new disclosures of truth
await them after their sudden transfer from
this scene of mental activity. One can
hardly have that feeling with regard to Mulford. The field of his thought was in this
world. He held that large conception of
eternity which was so vital a part of Maurice's teaching, — a conception which disregarded almost willfully any aid from the future ; his thought of prophecy left the predictive element quite out of view. He did
not reason concerning this world and the
next, but rather of this world as seen in its
universal relations, and the central truth of
his theology gave a sublimity to human nature which cast its glow over everything

which man cares for.   It is hard, as the saying is, to make him dead.   He does not belong among the dead.   His luminous nature
lives on, but it is the sorrowful fortune of
his friends that they live in the penumbra of
his memory, not in the glow of his presence.

LONGFELLOW AND HIS ART.

WHEN the history of civilization in America comes to be written, the judicious author will begin a consideration of the period which we are just now unwittingly closing, somewhat as follows : —

There was as yet no sign of any general interest in the graphic arts. Here and there a painter of portraits found a scanty recognition among families moved more by pride of station than by love of art, and a lonely painter of landscapes had tried to awaken enthusiasm for autumn scenes, which were taken to be the contribution of America to subjects in landscape art ; but such men escaped to Europe, if fortunate, and found a more congenial home there. Popular apprehension of art was wanting ; there was no public to which the painter could appeal with any confidence, nor indeed any public out of which a painter would naturally emerge. Then it was that a group of poets began to sing, having little personal connection with each other, forming no school, very diverse in aim, but all obedient to the laws of art. The effect upon the people was not confined to a development of the love of poetry; it was impossible that the form which art first took in America should be exclusive of other forms: on the contrary, poetry, the pioneer, led after it in rapid succession the graphic and constructive arts and music. Now we may trace this influence of poetry most distinctly in the case of Longfellow's work. Not only was his poetry itself instinct with artistic power, but his appropriating genius drew within the circle of his art a great variety of illustration and suggestion from the other arts. The subjects which he chose for his verse often compelled the interpretation of older examples of art. He had a catholic taste, and his rich decoration of simple themes was the most persuasive agency at work in familiarizing Americans with the treasures of art and legend in the Old World. Even when dealing expressly with American subjects, his mind was so stored with the abundance of a maturer civilization that he was constantly, by reference and allusion, carrying the reader on a voyage to Europe. Before museums were established in the cities, and before his countrymen had begun to go in shoals to the Old World, Longfellow had, in his verse, made them sharers in the riches of art. It is not too much to say that he was the most potent individual force for culture in America, and the rapid spread of taste and enthusiasm for art, which may be noted in the people near the end of his long and honorable career, may be referred more distinctly to his influence than to that of any other American.

So far our judicious historian, who has, as men of his class are apt to have, a weakness for periods and sounding phrases. Still a quotation from his forthcoming treatise does not seem wholly out of place as an introduction to an examination of those principles of art which controlled Longfellow, in his conscious and unconscious development of power. In studying his genius we have the double advantage of a chronological series of poems, and a tolerably continuous expression, by the poet, of his attitude toward his work, in the form of diaries and letters. His was one of those rare natures that perceive their destiny with distinctness from the time when consciousness makes them distinct persons. He knew as well in the last year of his college

life that he was meant for literature as he
did in the last year of his earthly life.   He
saw with clearness of poetic vision the meaning of his endowment, and with that fine
confidence in his destiny which is faith in
the unseen he steered for port.   Yet it is
important to note that not poetry but literature was to him first his vocation; that the
differentiation by which he finally devoted
himself exclusively to poetic art took place
slowly.   We get a glimpse of the early de-
termining spirit when we read the letter
which he wrote to his father from Brunswick,
in his eighteenth year.

"The fact is," he writes, after detailing
his immediate plans, — "and I will not dis-
guise it in the least, for I think I ought not,
— the fact is, I most eagerly aspire after
future eminence in literature; my whole
soul burns ardently for it, and every earthly
thought centres in it.   There may be something visionary in this, but I flatter myself
that I have prudence enough to keep my
enthusiasm from defeating its own object by
too great haste.   Surely, there never was a
better opportunity offered for exertion of literary talent in our own country than is now
offered.   To be sure, most of our literary

men thus far have not been professedly so, until they have studied and entered the practice of theology, law, or medicine. But this is evidently lost time. I do believe that we ought to pay more attention to the opinion of philosophers, that 'nothing but nature can qualify a man for knowledge.' Whether nature has given me any capacity for knowledge or not, she has, at any rate, given me a very strong predilection for literary pursuits; and I am almost confident in believing that, if I can ever rise in the world, it must be by the exercise of my talent in the wide field of literature. With such a belief, I must say that I am unwilling to engage in the study of the law. . . . Let me reside one year at Cambridge; let me study *belles-lettres*, and after that time it will not require a spirit of prophecy to predict with some degree of certainty what kind of a figure I could make in the literary world."

This was the eager outlook of a young man who uses some of the conventional phrases of youth, and puts forward the plea which a son thinks will be operative with a father; but there is an unmistakably genuine ring to the expression of faith in his calling, and the resolution which he showed in the

next few years, when he was qualifying himself ostensibly for the post of professor, but
quite consciously for the larger field of literature, disclosed a strong nature not afflicted
by petty doubts.   The testimony of a friend
affords a further glimpse of the young poet
when he was comprehending more fully the
power which he held. Mr. George W. Greene,
in dedicating his *The Life of Nathanael
Greene* to Longfellow, recalls an evening in
Naples when the two friends were drawn
into mutual confidences.

" We wanted," he says, " to be alone, and
yet to feel that there was life all around us.
We went up to the flat roof of the house,
where, as we walked, we could look down
into the crowded street, and out upon the
wonderful bay, and across the bay to Ischia
and Capri and Sorrento, and over the house-
tops and villas and vineyards to Vesuvius.
The ominous pillar of smoke hung suspended
above the fatal mountain, reminding us of
Pliny, its first and noblest victim. A golden
vapor crowned the bold promontory of Sorrento, and we thought of Tasso. Capri was
calmly sleeping, like a sea-bird upon the
waters; and we seemed to hear the voice of
Tacitus from across the gulf of eighteen cen-

turies, telling us that the historian's pen is still powerful to absolve or to condemn long after the imperial sceptre has fallen from the withered hand.   There, too, lay the native island of him whose daring mind conceived the fearful vengeance of the Sicilian Vespers.   We did not yet know Niccolini ; but his grand verses had already begun their work of regeneration in the Italian heart. Virgil's tomb was not far off.   The spot consecrated by Sannazaro's ashes was near us. And over all, with a thrill like that of solemn music, fell the splendor of the Italian sunset.

" We talked and mused by turns, till the twilight deepened and the stars came forth to mingle their mysterious influences with the overmastering magic of the scene.   It was then that you unfolded to me your plans of life, and showed me from what 'deep cisterns' you had already learned to draw. From that day the office of literature took a new place in my thoughts.   I felt its forming power as I had never felt it before, and began to look with a calm resignation upon its trials, and with true appreciation upon its rewards.   Thenceforth, little as I have done of what I wished to do, literature has been the inspiration, the guide, and the comfort of my life."

This was in 1828, and not long after Longfellow was writing home : " My poetic career is finished. Since I left America I have hardly put two lines together." It could not, therefore, have been the prophecy of a distinctly poetic vocation which so deeply moved Greene ; it must rather have been that Longfellow, after two years' travel and study in Europe, and when looking forward to definite academic work in America, was forecasting a life devoted to literary art, in which poetry was not the predominant element. When a collegian he had won his little reputation almost exclusively as a poet. To his friends, watching him across the water, that was his character, and it was no doubt in answer to natural inquiries that he declared his poetic career finished. That he was sincere in this belief is clearly seen by the entry in his note-book, at this time, of the subjects upon which he proposed at once to write. They were all of them planned for prose treatment, and, what is even more noticeable, they were drawn from American life and history.

It is customary to speak of Longfellow as

if his Americanism was an accident, his natural disposition leading him really to an
emigration in thought and sentiment to the
other side of the Atlantic.   In point of fact,
he passed through the experience of many
ingenuous American youth.   He ardently
desired an introduction to the Old World;
he entered quickly and warmly into the
spirit of the past, but instead of losing himself in this spirit, he found himself; he took
his spiritual bearings, and as a result set his
face more positively westward than could
have been possible had he never gone
through the process of orientation.   It is a
superficial judgment which determines the
nationality of a literary artist by his choice
of subjects alone.   Longfellow in Europe,
jotting down in his diary subjects drawn
from life in the Maine woods, was no more
essentially American than he was essentially
European when he was sitting in his study
in Brunswick and writing *Outre-Mer*.   The
residence in Europe made him eager for
his American life; the return to America
brought back with a rush the recollection of
European scenes.   In both cases the artist
was employing the convenient perspective of
time and space.   What was remote shaped

itself more definitely into picturesque relations to his mind; only to the student just
returned from Europe, after three years of
incessant occupation with new and suggestive forms of life and art, his own personal
experience offers so rich and tumultuous a
collection of themes that all else is for the
time held in abeyance.

This was markedly true in Longfellow's
case, because his mind by natural disposition
busied itself with the secondary rather than
with the primary facts of nature and society.
He was born and trained until he was nine-
teen in a society and amidst scenes exceedingly simple, almost elemental, indeed. No
one can read the chapters in his *Life* which
deal with his home in Portland and his education at Bowdoin College, — especially no
one can have recollection of the primitive,
provincial period of New England which had
its culmination just before the first steamer
crossed the Atlantic, — without perceiving
how much had been eliminated from the
American variation of the English mind by
the absence for two centuries of familiar contact with university, cathedral, castle, theatre,
gallery, and barracks. The brick college, the
wooden meeting-house, the merchant's square-

built house, the singing-school, the peripatetic Greek Slave, the muster, — all these marked the limits of expression, and by consequence the strength of reacting influence. The effect upon individual minds differed according to the original constitution of those minds. Hawthorne, gathering blueberries under the pines of Brunswick with his friend Bridge, was subjected to very much the same influences as Longfellow. He went out into the world later, it is true, than his great contemporary, but the author of *The Scarlet Letter* did not need to draw his breath of inspiration from any mediæval chronicle or under the shadow of Strasburg Cathedral; an old newspaper in the Salem Custom-House was enough for him. Longfellow, on the other hand, was writing of Italian scenery and Venetian gondoliers when his visits to Italy and Venice had been only in boats with sails rigged from the leaves of books. Even when treating of distinctly American subjects, as in the poem of *The Indian Hunter*, he borrowed his expression from traditions of English poetry : —

> " The foot of the reaper moved slow on the lawn,
>   And the sickle cut down the yellow corn ;
>   The mower sung loud by the meadow-side,

> Where the mists of evening were spreading wide;
> And the voice of the herdsmen came up by the lea,
> And the dance went round by the greenwood tree.''

Was all that the result of observations on a Maine farm? No; it indicates a mind sensitive to poetic influences as derived not so much from direct contact with nature as from indirect acquaintance through books. It is doubtful if there is a single line in the poems written before his journey to Europe which describes an aspect of nature specifically noted by the poet, unless it be two or three lines in his poem *Autumn*, where he says : —

> " The purple finch,
> That on wild cherry and red cedar feeds,
> A winter bird, comes with its plaintive whistle,
> And pecks by the witch-hazel; "

while there are repeated instances of entirely second-hand reflections of scenes which were impossible to his eye, as when, in his poem *To Ianthe*, he says : —

> " As I mark the moss-grown spring
>   By the twisted holly,''

and,

> " Twisted close the ivy clings
>   To the oak that 's hoarest."

Even when dealing with a slight historic fact, as in the *Hymn of the Moravian Nuns*

of Bethlehem, he translates the entire incident into terms of foreign import.   The dy-
ing flame of day shoots its ray through the
chancel; the glimmering tapers shed faint
light on the cowled head; the burning cen-
ser swings before the altar; the nuns' sweet
hymn is sung low in the dim, mysterious
aisle.   Yet the poem, masquerading in foreign dress, has a native fire and an enthusiasm kindled by the thought of personal
sacrifice in a great cause.   So, too, in the
Burial of the Minnisink, where the red
chief is only a mere transliteration of mediæval knight, the poetic passion flames forth
in a single bold phrase at the end of the
poem : —

> " They buried the dark chief ; they freed
>   Beside the grave his battle steed ;
>   And swift an arrow cleaved its way
>   To his stern heart !   One piercing neigh
>   Arose, and, on the dead man's plain,
>   The rider grasps his steed again."

It may be said, therefore, with some confidence that Longfellow's mental growth was
accelerated, not changed, by his study in
Europe ; that the bent of his genius was toward the artistic use of the reflected forms
of nature and of the product of human forces ;

that he sought instinctively for those expressions of life which had color and richness, not for those which had elemental significance; and that, failing to note such expressions in the life about him, he endowed the scenes which he depicted with qualities borrowed from an older, more complex civilization. The very sober needlewomen of the Moravian sisterhood were seen through painted glass; the squaws who sold baskets in Portland became a dark‑haired virgin train, chanting the death dirge of the slain; and it is only an anthropologist, accustomed to the meagre results of an exploration among mounds, who will at first glance detect the plain truth concerning the savage, when he reads : —

> "A dark cloak of the roebuck's skin
> Covered the warrior, and within
> Its heavy folds the weapons, made
> For the hard toils of war, were laid;
> The cuirass, woven of plaited reeds,
> And the broad belt of shells and beads."

A Norse viking stood in the light of an Old-town Indian, when the poet was sketching.

It was to a mind thus sensitive to rich color and complex form, and restrained from large opportunities during its adolescence, that a three years' wandering through Europe

brought a fullness of experience which enlarged and strengthened it, and not merely
supplied it with new objects of exercise.
Why was it that, after writing verse with
pleasure for two or three years, Longfellow
should suddenly drop the occupation, declare
his poetic career finished, and devote himself
assiduously to prose?   And why, to antici-
pate a further development, did he then return to prose deliberately but once more
after another decade?   From 1824 to 1826
he was writing those poems which are classed
as juvenile or earlier poems.   From 1831 to
1838 he wrote the bulk of his miscellaneous
prose and *Outre-Mer* and *Hyperion.*   In
1838 he resumed his poetic career with
Flowers and *A Psalm of Life,* and in 1848
he wrote *Kavanagh.*

I have half answered the first question already.   When he went to Europe in 1826,
it was ostensibly to qualify himself for the
post of professor of modern languages in
Bowdoin College.   Immediately, to use the
energetic phrase, his eyes were opened, and
in seeing the rich deposit of an old civilization, where history had for centuries been
building a house for the imagination, he was
conscious of power, he found himself.   Yet

he needed time for the thorough orientation
which his nature demanded.   There are
some poets who become naturalized in antiquity as soon as they land after their first
voyage. Keats was one of these.   There
are others who, if they take out their papers
early, do not at once exercise the rights of
citizenship, and Longfellow was one of these.
The period between his first emigration to
Europe, in 1826, and his final settlement at
Cambridge, in 1836, was one of accumula-
tion and disposition of his treasures.   The
circumstances of his outer life, his successive journeys for specific purpose, his brief
trial of teaching at Bowdoin, his experiments
in literature, corresponded with the internal
adjustment of his mind to its vocation.   It
was his apprentice time, and only when *Hyperion* was executed did he feel within himself that he had become a master.

His prose during this decade indicates
very clearly his spiritual and artistic growth.
He had come, by travel and study, into possession of a great store of material, the value
of which he was ready to discern. He was
laying then the foundation of that familiar
acquaintance with the localities of legend and
song and literary art, which gave to all his

work, so far as it was allusive of art, a light-
ness of touch, a confidence and an affection-
ateness of handling. It took him ten years,
however, to make all this material really his
own ; he began the process by simple description, and prose was his natural vehicle.
His letters show how quickly he caught the
spirit of what he saw, and a comparison
of *Outre-Mer* with them indicates the presence in his mind of a distinct literary sense.
One may prefer the directness of the letters,
but cannot help seeing that when Longfellow
set up the same material in his book he was
studying the form of presentation, and recognized that literature was something other
than letter-writing. Along with and following *Outre-Mer* were those special studies of
modern language and literature which confessed the student rather than the traveller ;
and then came *Hyperion*, in which the imaginative constructive power began to reassert
itself, and all the aspects of life and literature which had met the eye of the traveller
and student were considered by the poetic
mind and the creative genius. As has been
so often pointed out, the tale is a rescript,
only slightly disguised, of the poet's spiritual
as well as external experience ; but only

when one considers it as the final outcome of
a period of mental reconstruction does one
apprehend the entire significance of the work.
It marks the completion of Longfellow's apprenticeship to literature, and, like most
such critical works, it is as prophetic as it
is historical.

When, shortly after the publication of
Hyperion, Longfellow suddenly resolved to
publish a volume of poems, it may be fairly
assumed that he was in no sense renouncing
prose, but only thinking of himself as an
active *littérateur*, who was not shut up to
any one form of expression. He was not
yet, indeed, so conscious of his destiny that
he could not outline, a few days later, a plan
of literary work which embraced a history of
English poetry, a novel, a series of sketches,
and only one poem. His resolution to issue
Voices of the Night undoubtedly sprang
from the growing recognition of his poetic
faculty. He was still a student, but the ur-
gency of the student - mood was passed ; the
riches of human thought had become in a
measure his possession ; his personal experience had been enlarged and deepened ; he
no longer saw principally the outside of the
world ; youth with its surrender to the mo-

ment had gone, and manhood with its hours of reflection had come. So we may interpret the poet's mood as it discloses itself in the verses which introduce his first volume of original poetry.

But this little book offers a significant clue to the interpretation of the poet's art. In *L'Envoi*, which closes the book and serves as a poetic summary of its contents, he speaks of —

> " Tongues of the dead, not lost,
>   But speaking from Death's frost,
>   Like fiery tongues at Pentecost ! "

In truth, one of the most interesting phases of the apprenticeship to literature which Longfellow passed through was the manner in which he kept alive that spark of poetic fire which, feeble enough in his adolescence, was yet genuine. In the same letter in which he wrote to his sister, " My poetic career is finished," he attempted a translation of a lovely little Portuguese song, and as soon as he began his series of prose writings he began also that series of translations which would alone have given him the name of poet. It was necessary, in the course of his critical work, to give examples of verse, and he was thus constantly impelled to use

the metrical form; then when he essayed
the romance form, and cast his scenes largely in Germany, the very structure of his
work called for those "flowers of song"
which were the essential expression of the
life which he was translating into artistic
mode.

Throughout his life Longfellow found in
the work of translation a gentle stimulus to
his poetic faculty, and resorted to it when he
wished to quicken his spirit. "I agree with
you entirely," he writes to Freiligrath, November 24, 1843, "in what you say about
translations. It is like running a plough-
share through the soil of one's mind; a thousand germs of thought start up (excuse this
agricultural figure), which otherwise might
have lain and rotted in the ground. Still,
it sometimes seems to me like an excuse for
being lazy, — like leaning on another man's
shoulder." This is, however, but a partial
explanation of the place which translation
held in Longfellow's art. One must go back
to the very nature of this poet to see why it
is that so large a proportion of his poetical
work was either direct translation or a reconstruction from foreign material. In the
complete edition of his writings, three of the

nine volumes of poetry are given to the translation of Dante, with, to be sure, the volu-
minous apparatus of notes and illustrations,
while of another volume about two thirds of
the matter consist of translations from various languages. But the longest section of
Tales of a Wayside Inn, the *Musician's
Tale of the Saga of King Olaf*, is scarcely
other than a paraphrase ; *The Mother's
Ghost*, in the same book, is openly from the
Danish; and *Christus*, *Judas Maccabœus*,
and *Michael Angelo* are largely indebted
to other forms of literature for their very
phrases. It would not be difficult for one,
running through the entire body of poems,
to find in those relating to foreign subjects
a constant indirect reference to existing literary material. Not only so, but in such
poems as *The Courtship of Miles Standish*
and *Evangeline* the scaffolding which the
poet used could easily be put up again by
the historical student; of the *Tales of a
Wayside Inn*, only one is in any peculiar
sense the poet's invention ; while *Hiawatha*
is Schoolcraft translated into poetry.

It is when one enlarges the conception of
the word "translation" that one perceives
the value as well as the limitations of Long-

fellow's art.   He was a consummate translator, because the vision and faculty divine
which he possessed was directed toward the
reflection of the facts of nature and society,
rather than toward the facts themselves.
He was like one who sees a landscape in
a Claude Lorraine glass; by some subtle
power of the mirror everything has been com-
posed for him.   Thus, when he came to use
the rich material of history, of poetry, and of
other arts, Longfellow saw these in forms
already existing, and his art was not so much
a reconstruction out of crude material as a
representation, a rearrangement, in his own
exquisite language, of what he found and admired.   He was first of all a composer, and
he saw his subjects in their relations rather
than in their essence.   To tell over again
old tales, to reproduce in forms of delicate
fitness the scenes and narratives which others
had invented, — this was his delight; for in
doing this he was conscious of his power and
he worked with ease.   Thus it is that the lyrical translations which he made in his student days are really his own poems; he rendered the foreign form in a perfect English
form; his work in this regard was that of
an engraver, not that of a photographer.

He has himself said on the general subject of translation : —

"The great art of translating well lies in the power of rendering literally the words of a foreign author, while at the same time we preserve the spirit of the original. But how far one of these requisites of a good translation may be sacrificed to the other, how far a translator is at liberty to embellish the original before him while clothing it in a new language, is a question which has been decided differently by persons of different tastes. The sculptor, when he transfers to the inanimate marble the form and features of a living being, may be said not only to copy, but to translate. But the sculptor cannot represent in marble the beauty and expression of the human eye; and in order to remedy this defect as far as possible, he is forced to transgress the rigid truth of nature. By sinking the eye deeper, and making the brow more prominent above it, he produces a stronger light and shade, and thus gives to the statue more of the spirit and life of the original than he could have done by an exact copy. So, too, the translator."

In that which was technically translation, then, Longfellow made the foreign poems his own without sacrificing the truth of the originals; in that which was in a more general sense translation, the transfer, namely, of the spirit rather than the precise form of foreign art, he preserved the essential quality of what he took so perfectly as to lead many to underestimate the value of his own share in the result. Yet this fine sense of form, this intuitive perception of fitness, was an inestimable endowment of the artist, and is one of his passports to immortality. It is, however, most appreciable in those forms of art which are least dependent upon passion and more allied with the common experience; in dramatic art it has less significance. The use of the hexameter in *Evangeline* and the adoption of the *Kalevala* measure in *Hiawatha* are illustrations of how a great artist will choose forms perfectly fitted to his purpose, yet exceedingly dangerous in the hands of less skillful workmen. The pathway of English poetry is strewn with bones of hexametrical beasts of burden, but Longfellow's *Evangeline* has made the journey to the present time with every prospect of carrying her rider to the gates of whatever blessed country of immunity from criticism awaits the poet. An interesting illustration of Longfellow's unerring sense of form is fur-

nished by a trifling experiment which he
made when engaged upon *Evangeline*. He
records in his diary the completion of the
second canto of Part II., and adds, "I tried
a passage of it in the common rhymed English pentameter. It is the song of the mocking-bird : —

"Upon a spray that overhung the stream,
    The mocking-bird, awaking from his dream,
    Poured such delirious music from his throat
    That all the air seemed listening to his note.
    Plaintive at first the song began, and slow;
    It breathed of sadness, and of pain, and woe ;
    Then, gathering all his notes, abroad he flung
    The multitudinous music from his tongue, —
    As, after showers, a sudden gust again
    Upon the leaves shakes down the rattling rain."

Taken by itself this verse falls agreeably on
the ear, but it needs only a moment's thought
to perceive that the story of Evangeline
given in this measure would have been robbed
of that lingering melancholy, that pathos of
lengthening shadows, which resides in the
hexameter as Longfellow has handled it.
Something of all this may be seen even in
the few lines of the poem which render the
passage just given : —

"Then from a neighboring thicket the mocking-bird,
        wildest of singers,
    Swinging aloft on a willow spray that hung o'er the
        water,

Shook from his little throat such floods of delirious
    music

That the whole air and the woods and the waves seemed
    silent to listen.

Plaintive at first were the tones and sad ; then soaring
    to madness

Seemed they to follow or guide the revel of frenzied
    Bacchantes.

Single notes were then heard, in sorrowful, low lamen-
    tation ;

Till, having gathered them all, he flung them abroad
    in derision,

As when, after a storm, a gust of wind through the
    tree-tops

Shakes down the rattling rain in a crystal shower on
    the branches.''

The limitations of the rhymed pentameter
are clearly seen in a comparison of the two
forms, — its limitations, and also its brief
gain, for as the expression of a single moment the shorter form is more immediate in
its operation. One catches the incident on
the wing, instead of watching it slowly from
inception to close, and I suspect that Longfellow may have been led to make this little
experiment from a perception, as he wrote
the hexameters, of the slight loss thereby
sustained ; if so, it is only another illustration of his exquisite sense of form.

The deliberate note which a poet strikes
at the outset of his career may wisely be

taken as indicative of his conscious judgment of his own vocation. Although, as we have seen, Longfellow grew into poetry through the exercise of translation, and by a decade of fruitful study acquired that mastery of form which fixed his place in literature primarily as an artist, it is equally true that the spirit which in youth at once chose poetry as expression was not changed, but only held in reserve through the formative period, and as soon as true maturity came broke forth once more in its native language. The *Prelude* which opens *Voices of the Night* and *L'Envoi* which closes the volume together disclose the poet's attitude toward his verse. He had gathered his recent poems, and chosen from his scattered translations and his earlier work such examples as came nearest to his more educated taste, and now proposed sending them out into the world. The very title of the volume hinted at the poet's mood. From the *Orestes* of Euripides he took his motto, and paraphrased it in the last stanza of the opening poem, *Hymn to the Night:* —

"Peace! Peace! Orestes-like I breathe this prayer!
    Descend with broad-winged flight,
  The welcome, the thrice-prayed for, the most fair,
    The best-beloved Night!"

The title *Voices of the Night* was first given
to the poem *Footsteps of Angels*, and all of
the poems in the section, that is, all the
poems which sprang from the new birth of
poetry in his mind, strike a single key, —
that of consolation; and so full is the poet
of this sense of his poetic mission that he
breaks forth at the close of his *Prelude* in
these words, catching, characteristically, at a
phrase of Sir Philip Sidney's: —

> "Look, then, into thine heart, and write!
>   Yes, into Life's deep stream!
> All forms of sorrow and delight,
> All solemn Voices of the Night,
> That can soothe thee, or affright,
>   Be these henceforth thy theme."

There is no doubt that the poet's personal
history in the period immediately preceding
the appearance of *A Psalm of Life* and
similar poems had much to do with this
mood, and certainly this "theme" was by no
means thenceforth his only one, although it
reappeared frequently. It was natural, also,
that his recent study of Jean Paul and
other sentimental Germans should affect his
choice and treatment of subjects, but there is
a deeper, more fundamental account. Longfellow's nature was one of religious bent; his
training had been that of the liberal school,

and his interest in institutional, historical Christianity was rather æsthetic than inbred. He was also a man of deep reserve, and shrank not only from the disclosure of his intimate feeling, but generally from all revelation of sacred experience. He found in poetry a form of expression which permitted great freedom of speech without necessary reference to the personality of the author. Behind this almost transparent screen he could give full utterance to his own interior life, all the while appearing as the priest of humanity. It was not his own loss which he registered in *Resignation,* although the occasion of the poem came from his own loss; but he generalized his grief, and took refuge in his office as spokesman for the crowd of sorrowful ones. Thus his personal outlook supplied the fervor of *A Psalm of Life,* and infused into those lines of commonplaces a poetic spirit which makes them have the sound of a trumpet call; but the lines could not be tracked home to their author by any clue which his personal history might furnish. His home, his friends, the multitudinous experience in emotion of a sensitive nature, constantly supplied him with impulses to poetic expression, but he spoke for himself and others, very rarely for himself alone.

It was for this reason, in part, that he seized so readily upon the symbols of religion which he found in historic Christianity, and made use of them as forms in his poetic art. His delight in *The Golden Legend* was not only an artist's pleasure in rich color and form, but the pleasure of a religious nature working in material that allowed full scope to motives born of religious faith. The remark of Ruskin, often quoted, that " Longfellow, in his *Golden Legend*, has entered more closely into the temper of the monk, for good and for evil, than ever yet theological writer or historian, though they may have given their life's labor to the analysis," is in support of this view. Longfellow read the monk as he read all mediæval Christianity, from the vantage of a man sympathetic with religion in whatever sincere form it took, unembarrassed by any personal concern in the church which enshrined this particular faith, and keenly sensitive to whatever filled the imagination ; while, as a poet, and especially as a poet of high order as composer, he was able to select just those noble and essential features which justify claims to reverence and admiration, and to oppose as shades those features which could be regarded as transient and accidental.

How important an element in Longfellow's art was his religious feeling appears when one considers the two works which dominated his life. I have said that the deliberate note which a poet strikes at the beginning of his career ought to be heeded for the disclosure which it makes of his consciousness of vocation ; and the psalms of life which stirred Longfellow's spirit, as he once more found expression in poetry, showed him as a priest of humanity ; they were indicative of a nature religious, emotional, reserved, yet eagerly desirous of translating his discovery of himself into the broad, universal terms. The time from 1837 to 1841, marked in his life by the entrance upon residence at Cambridge, with its duties in teaching not yet irksome, was a period of quick poetic exercise and the trial of a variety of forms. It saw, besides the *Voices of the Night*, experiments in ballads, like *The Wreck of the Hesperus* and *The Skeleton in Armor* ; a drama, *The Spanish Student* ; his famous poem, *Excelsior*, in which his art executed its most splendid feat in bridging the gulf between the sublime and the ridiculous; and it offers to the reader of his life a picture of spirited youth, weighted, indeed, by physical infirmity, but with the foot in the stirrup. Yet of what was he thinking? What was he planning to do? It was near the close of 1841 that he wrote in his diary: —

"This evening it has come into my mind to undertake a long and elaborate poem by the holy name of Christ, the theme of which would be the various aspects of Christendom in the Apostolic, Middle, and Modern Ages;" and he adds, characteristically using a quotation to express his own deepest thought, "And the swete smoke of the odorous incense whych came of the wholesome and fervent desyres of them that had fayth ascended up before God, out of the aungel's hande."

It was not till 1873 that the work as it now stands was published; and for those two and thirty years which represent almost the whole of his productive period the subject of the trilogy seems never to have been long absent from his mind. As I have said elsewhere, the theme, in its majesty, was a flame by night and a pillar of cloud by day, which led his mind in all its onward movement, and he esteemed the work which he had undertaken as the really great work of his life. His religious nature was profoundly moved by it, and the degree of doubt which attended every step of his progress marked the height of the endeavor which he put forth. There was nothing violent or eccentric in this sudden resolution. The entry in his journal, his biographer states, is the only one for that year, but his correspondence and the dates of his poems indicate clearly enough that the course of his mental and spiritual life was flowing in a direction which made this resolve a most natural and at the same time inspiring expression of his personality. He had been singing those psalms of life, triumphant, sympathetic, aspiring, which showed how strong a hold the ethical principle had of him; he had been steeping his soul in Dante; he had been moved by the tender ecclesiasticism of *The Children of the Lord's Supper*, and in recording a passage in the life of Christ had fancied himself a monk of the Middle Ages; while the whole tenor of his life and thought had shown how strong a personal apprehension he had of the divine in humanity.

In all that calls for delicate taste, a fine

sense of fitness, and a skillful use of material
already formed, this trilogy, like the other
dramatic writings of Longfellow, has the
poet's distinctive mark.   In no part is this
more clear than in *The Divine Tragedy.*   A
large portion of this drama is a deftly arranged mosaic of passages from the evangel-
ists, and the reader is at first quite as much
struck with the rhythmical character of the
King James version, which permits the
words to fall so easily into the metrical
order, as he is with the poet's skill in selection and adjustment.   Probably the indifference shown by people in general to this
drama is due in part to the feeling that nothing very novel was offered.   In fact, Longfellow's reverence is sufficient to explain his
lack of success.   The desire which he had
to accomplish the great work of *Christus*
sprang not only from a poet's conception of
the great movement involved in the subject,
but from a deep sense of personal obliga-
tion.   He approached this dramatic representation of the Christ somewhat as a painter
might propose a Crucifixion as a votive offering, only that while the painter, in a great
period of religious art, would be working in
a perfectly well understood and accepted

mode, this poet was artistically alone, and was not merely not helped, but actually hindered by the prevalent religious temper. Thorwaldsen's Christ is an example of how an artist, unincumbered by too strong a personal feeling, is able to avail himself of the sympathy of his fellow-believers. The statue, repeated large and small, has become the type of Lutheran Protestant Christianity; but it has become so because its sculptor drew from Lutheranism his conception of the Christ, not so much as the Sufferer as the Friend. Longfellow, on the other hand, has added nothing to the New England conception of the Christ, because he neither met the requirements of the traditional faith which concentrated all the drama into one act, nor was able to precipitate the floating views of the liberal theology into so striking a dramatic form as to present a figure which would be recognized as the one that men were looking for. Perhaps that was too much to ask under any circumstances, and certainly, as a human hero of a drama, a more disappointing subject could not be found than the Man of Nazareth. At any rate, Longfellow was not the one to lay sacrilegious hands on the ark of his own hopes, and he could not as an artist deny himself as a reverent believer.

After all, the very presence of those qualities which we have observed in Longfellow's art seems to exclude the admission of that requisite to dramatic art, — passion. The graces which enrich the lyrical and narrative work are somewhat foreign from the drama. One needs to break bounds there, the bounds not of law, but of conventions, and the most orderly and reasonable succession of scenes can hardly put the reader into that state of forgetfulness of self which the drama should compel. There is one scene in *Judas Maccabœus*, where the mother of the seven sons listens to the voices of her children as they undergo torments in the dungeon of the citadel, which is conceived with fine force; and yet, upon closer examination, one is obliged to concede that Longfellow was here displaying not so much dramatic conception as that admirable faculty in the adjustment and arrangement of forms already at hand to which I have several times referred.

The question was asked incidentally, on a previous page, why, after once abandoning prose at the end of a decade of work in it, Longfellow should return to prose after another decade given almost wholly to poetry. In 1838 *Hyperion* was written, and was followed at once by *Voices of the Night*. In 1848 *Kavanagh* appeared, and was the last piece of prose produced by the author. It stands in the midst also of a poetic period: *Evangeline* had just been finished, and *The Golden Legend* was begun shortly after *Kavanagh* was published, while the volume *The Seaside and the Fireside* collected a number of noticeable short poems.

It is probable that in writing *Kavanagh* Longfellow was obeying an impulse which often seizes artists, to lay at rest some ghost of a purpose that has pursued them. In his earliest plans for literary work, made on his first journey to Europe, he had outlined several sketches of American life. He made one or two essays in this direction after his return, but hid them away in annuals so carefully that only recently have they been unearthed. He was also somewhat in love with the character of a country schoolmaster, since it seemed to furnish the opportunity for combining the two elements of a recluse and a man of learning and taste. Then he could not help having his opinions about the national literature which was exercising the

writers of his day, and as in *Hyperion* he
had disclosed something of his personal life
under the veil of a romance, so in *Kavanagh*
he made a pleasing rural story the vehicle
for carrying reflections and opinions which
he wished once for all to be rid of.   He had
done with reviewing and prose work in general; whatever he did now must be in some
form of art, and *Kavanagh* seems to have
answered its purpose of materializing the
floating forms which had been in its author's
vision for many years.   After this he used
the economy of a wise artist, and worked in
that material and in those forms which most
completely satisfied the bent of his genius.

Yet *Kavanagh*, in another aspect, is interesting for its witness to a controlling principle in Longfellow's art.   When Michael
Angelo, in Longfellow's posthumous poem,
holds discourse from the vantage-ground of
age with the volatile Benvenuto Cellini, his
counsel to the younger man is mingled with
pathetic reflections upon his own relations to
art.   He cannot leave Rome for Florence;
he is under the spell which affects one like
malaria : —

> " Malaria of the mind
> Out of this tomb of the majestic Past ;

The fever to accomplish some great work
That will not let us sleep.   I must go on
Until I die.''

So he speaks, and to Benvenuto's reminder
of the memories which cluster about the
pleasant city upon the Arno, he replies,
musing : —

                     '' Pleasantly
Come back to me the days when, as a youth,
I walked with Ghirlandajo in the gardens
Of Medici, and saw the antique statues,
The forms august of gods and godlike men,
And the great world of art revealed itself
To my young eyes.   Then all that man hath **done**
Seemed possible to me.   Alas ! how little
Of all I dreamed of has my hand achieved ! ''

The caution against mistaking a poet's
dramatic assumption for his own character
and expression is of less force in the case
of one in whom the dramatic power was so
slightly developed ; and the whole poem of
Michael Angelo, taken in connection with
the time and circumstances of its composition, may fairly be regarded as in some respects Longfellow's *apologia pro vita sua.*
Michael Angelo rehearsing his art is dra-
matically conceived, and there is no lapse
into the poet's own speech ; for all that, and
because of that, the reader is always aware
of the presence of Longfellow, wise, calm,

reflective, musing over the large thoughts
of life and art. " I want it," the poet says
in his diary, " for a long and delightful occupation," and he treated himself to the
luxury of keeping the work by him, brooding over it, shaping it anew, adding, changing, discarding.

" Quickened are they that touch the Prophet's bones,"

he says in his *Dedication*, and it may easily
be believed that with no great scheme of
verse haunting him, with no sense of incom-
pleted plans, he would linger in the twilight
of his poetic life over the strong figure of
the artist thus called up before him, and be
kindled with a new poetic glow as he con-
templated the great artist. For Michael
Angelo in the poem is the virile character
of the robust Italian seen in a softened,
mellow light. We are not probably far
astray when we say that Longfellow, in
building this poem and reflecting upon it
during the last ten years of his life, was
more distinctly declaring his artistic creed
than in any other of his works, and that the
discussions which take place in the poem,
more especially Michael Angelo's utterances
on plastic or graphic art, had a peculiar in-

terest for him as bearing upon analogous doctrines of poetic art.

Now the great sculptor is made to speak in his old age of

> " The fever to accomplish some great work,
> That will not let us sleep."

If there was any such fever in Longfellow's case, as I think the writing of *Michael Angelo* intimates, there certainly was from the beginning of his career a most healthy and normal activity of life, which stirred him to the achievement of great works, in distinction from the familiar, frequent exercise of the poetic faculty. That lovely lyric, *The Arrow and the Song*, which might well stand as a prelude to Longfellow's shorter poems, is headed in the complete edition by an extract from the author's diary : " Before church wrote *The Arrow and the Song*, which came into my mind as I stood with my back to the fire, and glanced on to the paper with arrow's speed. Literally an improvisation." The spontaneity of his art is again and again illustrated by just such lyrics as this, and no one can follow these shorter flights of song in connection with Longfellow's life without being impressed by the ease with which they sped from his

bow and the directness of their aim. But
to see this is to see only one side of Longfellow's artistic power. One needs also to
keep in mind the seriousness with which he
regarded his art, and the clear purpose always in his mind to build large and strong.
It is not impossible that his several attempts
at dramatic composition may have been due
in part to this temper which impelled him
to use all his strength, and to justify his
gift of song by something more than swal-
low dips. *Hyperion* was necessary to his
mind, though he might have broken up
much of the work into independent, minor
sketches. Scarcely had he been reborn to
poetry before he was at work on *The Spanish Student*. He was then also projecting
Christus, and evidently feeling the weight
of the great theme. The length of time
which it remained in his mind is an illustration of the large circle on which his thought
sailed, and his poetic career is marked to
the end by the deliberate inception, elabora-
tion, and completion of great works.

There is an aspect of Longfellow's art
which especially interests men of letters. I
mean the relation which it bore to his liveli-
hood. In one of his letters, written when

leaving college, he intimates that if his father insists upon his adopting a profession, he may accept the law. "I can be a lawyer," he says; "this will support my real existence, literature an *ideal* one." As it turned out, he was able to earn his living by a pursuit which was more directly akin to literature. For about twenty-five years he was bound by the exacting duties of a professorship, first at Bowdoin, afterward at Harvard. When he came to retire at last from his chair in the university, he wrote in his diary: "I am now free! But there is a good deal of sadness in the feeling of separating one's self from one's former life."

This was the formal separation. The real cessation of college work had taken place a few months earlier. But in the diary of the closing years of his connection with the college there are many signs of a growing weariness and a desire to be relieved of irksome duties. His function as a professor seems always to have been subordinate in his own consciousness, but never to have been slighted. More than that, his literary faculty distinctly reënforced his professional power. Apparently he brought to his work in the college no special love of teaching, nor, so far as we can see, any special gift of exegesis ; he brought something, however, that was rare in his position and of great value, — a deep love of literature and that unacademic attitude toward his work which was a liberalizing power.

Nor, on the other hand, can we say that his work in the college was of serious disadvantage to him as a man of letters. It is probable that he found in poetry a relief from the routine of his life, and that the business which compelled him gave a certain stability to his course, making it possible for him to keep poetry always like a pure flame leading him forward. At any rate, it is to be observed that during these twenty-five years, naturally the most fruitful in a poet's life, he wrote the poems which fixed his place on Parnassus. It was just at the turning-point that he wrote *Hiawatha*, but he had already written *Evangeline*, and those poems of hope and confidence to which he gave the name of psalms.

Still, in relinquishing his position as professor, Longfellow was not simply consulting his personal ease ; he was obeying that law of his higher nature which bade him cast off all impediments to a free exercise of his power as an artist. We are told that he disliked everything violent, and that this hatred of noise was a trait of his character from earliest days. It is easy to believe this, for one cannot read his *Life* or study his works without being made aware of an atmosphere created by the poet himself. There was no mere avoidance of disturbing elements, nor was his serenity the result of favoring conditions; his nature asserted itself in a resolute compulsion of conditions, —

> " Annihilating all that's made
> To a green thought in a green shade."

" We lead but one life here on earth," he writes in his diary. " We must make that beautiful. And to do this, health and elasticity of mind are needful; and whatever endangers or impedes these must be avoided." This last entry lets a little light into the poet's temperament. That calm sweetness of spirit, which is so apparent in Longfellow, was an acquisition as well as an endowment. He deliberately chose and refrained according to a law in his members, and took clear cognizance of his nature and its tendencies.

In a word, he was a sane man. There

was a notable sanity about all his mode of life, and his attitude toward books and nature and men. It was the positive which attracted him, the achievement in literature, the large, seasonable gifts of the outer world, the men and women themselves who were behind the deeds and words which made them known. The books which he read, as noted in his journals, were the generous books; he wanted the best wine of thought, and he avoided criticism. He basked in sunshine; he watched the sky, and was alive to the great sights and sounds and to all the tender influences of the seasons. In his intercourse with men, this sanity appeared in the power which he showed of preserving his own individuality in the midst of constant pressure from all sides; he gave of himself freely to his intimate friends, but he dwelt, nevertheless, in a charmed circle, beyond the lines of which men could not penetrate. Praise did not make him arrogant or vain; criticism, though it sometimes wounded him, did not turn him from his course. It is rare that one in our time has been the centre of so much admiration, and still rarer that one has preserved in the midst of it all that integrity of nature which never abdicates.

It is too early to make a full survey of
the immense importance to American letters
of the work done by half a dozen great men
in the middle of this century. The body of
prose and verse created by them is constituting the solid foundation upon which other
structures are to rise ; the humanity which
it holds is entering into the life of the country, and no material invention, or scientific
discovery, or institutional prosperity, or ac-
cumulation of wealth will so powerfully affect the spiritual well-being of the nation for
generations to come. The reason lies deep
in the lives of the men who have wrought,
independently, at laying this foundation. In
the case of Longfellow, the gift of nature
which made him an artist to his finger-tips
was reënforced by that broad, free study
which enriched his mind with a multitude
of familiar figures and forms, and behind
all lay a sane, reverent character which constantly obeyed the impulse to work, to create,
to be.

A MODERN PROPHET.

MR. FORD MADOX BROWN, in a large picture entitled *Work*, which he exhibited in London twenty years or more ago, introduced two figures, whom he thus described in the entertaining catalogue which accompanied his exhibition : " These are the brain-workers, who, seeming to be idle, work, and are the cause of well-ordained work and happiness in others. Sages, such as in ancient Greece, published their opinions in the market square. Perhaps one of these may already, before he or others know it, have moulded a nation to his pattern, converted a hitherto combative race to obstinate passivity ; with a word may have centupled the tide of emigration, with another have quenched the political passions of both factions, — may have reversed men's notions upon criminals, upon slavery, upon many things, and still be walking about little known to some. The other, in friendly communion with the philosopher, smiling, perhaps, at some of his

wild sallies and cynical thrusts (for Socrates
at times strangely disturbs the seriousness of
his auditory by the mercilessness of his jokes
— against vice and foolishness), is intended
for a kindred and yet very dissimilar spirit:
a clergyman, such as the Church of England
offers examples of, — a priest without guile,
a gentleman without pride, much in communion with the working classes, 'honoring all
men,' 'never weary in well-doing ;' scholar,
author, philosopher, and teacher, too, in his
way, but not above practical efforts, if even
for a small amount in good, deeply pene-
trated as he is with the axiom that each unit
of humanity feels as much as all the rest
combined, and impulsive and hopeful in nature, so that the remedy suggests itself to
him concurrently with the evil."

The former of these two characters, who
in the picture stand watching some navvies
at work, was Thomas Carlyle ; the latter,
Frederick Denison Maurice. The painter,
with that insight which belongs to his art,
associated two men who were, in point of
fact, not very closely connected in society,
yet who are likely to be mentioned in the
same breath by any one hereafter who takes
into account the individual spiritual forces

of modern England. It has been the fashion
to call Carlyle a new John the Baptist, and
it has been cleverly said that he led Englishmen into the desert and left them there.
If one chooses to push the comparison farther, and to say that he who is least in the
kingdom of heaven is greater than John the
Baptist, he will find in Maurice an exemplar
of the prophets who belong distinctly to the
new dispensation. Indeed, an enthusiastic
disciple has declared that the great distinction of Maurice was that he rediscovered
the gospel of the kingdom of heaven.   Herr
Brentano, the professor of political economy
at Strasburg, was of the opinion that Maurice
" was evidently marked out by his whole nature to exercise the influence of an apostle."
It is a more exact description of his function in modern English history to call him,
as I do, a prophet.

In using this term I bear in mind that
conception of prophecy which Maurice himself did so much in his writings to reclaim.
The difference between the large idea of
prophecy which prevailed in his mind and
that restricted notion which makes Mr. Ven-
nor or Zadkiel the chief of the prophets was
the difference of a single letter.   The popu-

lar view of a prophet is one who *fore tells ;*
that of Mr. Maurice, of the English theolo-
gians of the seventeenth century, and therefore of the translators of the Bible, was of
one who *for-tells.* The prophet, in their conception, is one who speaks for God ; and the
great function of the Jewish prophets was
not to furnish predictions which should at
some future time be fulfilled and astonish
skeptics, but to declare that mind of God
which rests in eternal righteousness and ex-
presses itself through the workings of human
will. That prophecy should have its predictive side is a consequence of the immu-
table properties of the divine nature and the
freedom of the human. The word of God
must have its final expression in man's conduct ; but it is not a thaumaturgic word, and
the process by which it accomplishes its ends
is a process in time.

It is the first condition of true prophecy
that the prophet himself should be conscious
of his vocation, and therefore of the God
who uses him for a mouthpiece. Out of this
consciousness of an immanent God springs
that double sense of profound humility and
unfaltering courage. The prophet is not a
passive instrument, a pipe for God's fingers

to sound what stops He pleases ; and yet the highest expression of prophetic power is accompanied by the most perfect subjection of the will.   Now Maurice was at once the most humble of men and the most confident in the delivery of his message from God to man. The whole course of his life reveals him as utterly indifferent to his own fame, social position, or personal advantage ; as wholly occupied with the great truths of God of which he was the recipient.   Woe is me, he seems always to be declaring, if I preach not the gospel ; but, unlike some who take up the same strain, it was not the gospel of woe which he felt constrained to preach.

The incidents of his life are easily summed. John Frederick Denison Maurice was born in 1805.   His father was a Unitarian minister whose character seems to have been cast somewhat in the mould in which the son's was formed.   Maurice was a student at Trinity College, Cambridge, where his tutor was Julius Hare and his bosom friend was John Sterling.   He did not take his degree, from conscientious scruples against signing the thirty-nine Articles, and went up to London, where he engaged in literary pursuits in company with Sterling.   Of Maurice's influence on Sterling, Sterling himself writes : " Of what good you have found in the *Athenæum* by far the larger part is attributable to Maurice. When I have done any good, I have seldom been more than a patch of sand to receive and retain the impression of his footsteps." Mulford once said to me that there were two Englishmen who might have written history to some purpose, De Quincey and Maurice. I suppose he was thinking of their insight, their power to detect the undercurrents of historic movement, a power which lets in a flood of light upon what otherwise seem unrelated facts. The *Athenæum* in noticing this period of Maurice's activity said : " Had Mr. Maurice finally resolved to abide in literature as his calling, he would have been the author of many rich suggestions and discoveries in the fields of criticism and history, and the world might have found in him a second Erasmus, but with a courage and faith and passionate devotion to truth, which are conspicuous by their absence in the first one."

Maurice knew himself better. He had no art, no sense of form, and without art a man of letters is without his distinctive mark. He had the genius of a worker, and it was in the ministry that he saw his most effective working-place. He entered the church, taking his degree at Oxford, for he had discovered, as he believed, an eirenicon in the Church of England, and thenceforward his work was within its pale, though he refused to accept the interpretation of the Church and its belief which were held by many of the Doctors of the Church. The school of thinking in which he would be placed received its special foundation, speculatively in Coleridge, practically in Arnold; and of those with whom he may be classed, Robertson, the brothers Hare, Tennyson, and Charles Kingsley are the most notable. He was successively chaplain of Guy's Hospital, chaplain of Lincoln's Inn, Incumbent of St. Peter's, Vere Street, and at the time of his death held the chair of Casuistry and Moral Philosophy in the University of Cambridge. He was also at one time Professor of Divinity in King's College, London, but was driven from his place by the theological opposition of the authorities. Much of his work was in connection with the Working Men's College of London.

His writings illustrate the leading interests of his life, for they may all be said to have been instruments which he handled for direct and specific purposes not containing the end in themselves. Their leading characteristic is the use of spiritual truths in the solution of problems of life, whether those problems are stated in terms of politics, religious and social observance, or morals. Indeed, nothing impresses one more in reading the writings of this man than the absence of customary boundary lines in thought. He has not one method for the investigation of scientific questions, and another for casuistry ; he does not regard politics and religion as independent and separate provinces of thought and action ; and therefore it is that in preaching to Englishmen, he speaks to Englishmen and not distinctively to members of the Church of England, any more than he would, if addressing a political gathering, speak to voters. Therefore it is also that his labors amongst working men always had a power springing from his recognition of them as a constituent part of the State, and not as members of a social class.

To speak briefly, Maurice shows in his writings a constant desire to get at the broad, fundamental experience of humanity. He recognizes social and religious differences in men only to point out more clearly the real likeness. What he has to say is said to his brethren; and exclusiveness, whether in religion or society, seems to him the gravest peril of Church or State. The practical temper of his mind led him to put his work into action, as I said, rather than into literature. His books are tracts, generally, rather than treatises, suggested by immediate needs, yet always bottomed on large, comprehensive principles. He is careless of mere scholastic distinctions; he writes to get at the heart of things. He uses literature for an end, and does not make an end of literature itself. One begins to read his writings with the expectation of finding eventually some definite system of thought to which they may be referred, but discovers at last that Maurice is not a systematic theologian; that he has positive conviction, a determinate faith, but has never formally abstracted it from its place as a motive power and given it a dogmatic shape. The personality of the man, hopeful and solemn, large and candid, yet sometimes sarcastic and slightly contemptuous, is impressed upon his writings and must have been a strong influence in the society which surrounded him.

He has been the cause of much thought in others, both in England and America, but I suspect his writings will be read less and less, while his personality will be studied more and more.

The main source of knowledge, as his contemporaries pass away, will probably be in the *Life*, based upon his correspondence, issued by his son, Colonel Frederick Maurice, who was in sympathy with his father. Colonel Maurice tells us that his father maintained that no man's life should be written until he had been dead twenty years. Maurice died ten years before the *Life* appeared, but for American readers the half score is as good as a score. We are sufficiently removed from the smoke of the battle in which so much of his life was spent to be able to view the combat with serenity, and the figure of this remarkable man becomes one of the most conspicuous in the scene. He was not a leader of a party; he was a leader of men. A keen Englishman who had boxed the compass of religious winds said sneeringly to me a few years ago that there were then only two out-and-out disciples of Maurice in London. Maurice himself would have been eager to dissuade the two from fancying that he carried any banner under which they could be marshalled.

To return to my preferable epithet, he was a prophet. What, then, was the message which this modern prophet delivered to men? It is discovered in every page of the books which he published, and is still further illustrated in a variety of forms in the *Life*. " His whole conception of preaching," says his biographer, " was the setting forth of Christ as the manifestation of the divine character; as the revelation, unveiling, or making known to man the actual righteousness and love of God. This was the gospel or good news which he believed that he had to preach. He believed that in proportion as men in private life or in history came to have a higher ideal of any kind, that ideal was in itself a more perfect knowledge of the nature of God, arrived at through the manifestation of the Son, the Word, in life or history." "I know I was formed," says Maurice himself, " in the image of God. I believe if I could behold God I should reflect His image. But I cannot behold Him. God, I am told, is a spirit, and I am of the earth, earthy. I cannot, and would not if I could, abandon my belief that He is a lofty

spiritual being ; I cannot throw aside my own
earthliness. Now this seems to me the most
important practical question in the world. I
cannot put up with a dream in place of God.
He is a spirit, but He is a reality ; a true
being in the highest sense. As such I must
behold Him, or not at all. To behold Him,
therefore, in that way in which they could
alone understand Him, in which they could
converse with Him, namely, as a man, was,
I see more and more clearly, the longing desire of every patriarch, prophet, and priest,
from Adam downward. It was the desire
of Moses, of Job, of David, of Solomon, of
Isaiah ; they were practical men, and they
wanted a practical revelation, — a revelation
which they could understand and grapple.
God, they knew, must be forever the un-
searchable, the mysterious. They would not
for worlds He should be anything else ; for
it was the glory of Judaism that their God
was not a visible, intelligible idol, but an
incomprehensible spirit. Yet they longed to
behold Him, and to behold Him so that they
could understand Him."

This concentration of his belief in God
rather than about God, and the intensity of
his conviction that God was revealed in the

incarnation, made Maurice a prophet, and
explains the whole course of his life. It explains his personal character, for the habit
of direct intercourse with its Deliverer afforded a test of conduct far more potent
than any code of ethics, however lofty. It
explains his attitude toward the Church, the
Bible, and, above all, toward the men and
women about him. It was impossible for
him to regard his personal relation to God
as an exclusive one. The very intensity of
his belief in God as the Father and in Christ
as the head of man made him have a passionate longing for a unity in the visible relations of men to one another which should
correspond to the eternal unity which sub-
sisted in the divine order. Hence his extreme sensitiveness to any course which
would identify him with party in Church or
State constantly isolated him from men with
whom he worked most cheerfully. It led
him into an almost morbid suppression of
himself, lest he should seem to be a leader.
"I am a cold-blooded animal," he writes to
Mr. Ludlow, who had reproved him in his
hasty way for checking the ardor of an associate ; " very incapable, I know, of entering
into the enthusiasm of better men, and often

likely to discourage them greatly. The consciousness of this often keeps me aloof from
them, as I feel I am doing them harm. But
I have sometimes thought that I might be of
use in warning those for whom I feel a deep
and strong interest against a tendency which
I feel in myself, and which I have seen producing most melancholy effects. I mean a
tendency to be quick-sighted in detecting all
errors in the schemes of other men, and to
set up their own in opposition to them. Oh,
the bitter scorn which I have seen Newman-
ites indulging at the schemes of Evangelicals ! — scorn in which I have been well in-
clined to join ; and now the frost which has
come on themselves, their incapacity of all
healthy action ! I could get the good-will of
you all very soon by flattering that habit of
mind, and I am very often tempted to do it.
But God will not let me, and therefore He
will not let me ever be the leader or sub-
leader of any school or party in this land.
For the only condition of the existence of
such a school or party is the denunciation
and execration of every other. I find myself
becoming more and more solitary. I see
that I am wide as the poles from Hare about
the baptismal question. He wishes to make

every one comfortable in the Church; and I
want no one to be comfortable in it, so cross-
grained am I. Yet I seek for unity in my
own wild way." " I have laid a great many
addled eggs in my time," he said once to his
son, " but I think I see a connection through
the whole of my life that I have only lately
begun to realize; the desire for unity and the
search after unity, both in the Nation and
the Church, has haunted me all my days."

The ideal which a man sets before him is
the measure of his life, if that ideal is never
shattered by the man's own loss of faith.
In Maurice's case, this search for unity was
carried on to the end, in spite of apparently
overwhelming odds. His early days were
spent in a religious society which was falling to pieces about him. His father's family went through a process of disintegration
of faith which is dramatic in its singular
rapidity and completeness. The figure of
the Rev. Michael Maurice, deserted in succession by all the members of his household,
is a most pathetic one. Yet all this experience lay at the basis of Frederick Maurice's
passionate devotion to his ideal. It was out
of this chaos that there arose in his mind a
conception of order which never failed him.

It centred in God, and found its expression
in those terms, the Word of God, the Family, the Nation, the Church, which were to
be constantly charged with a meaning in his
writings and speech that made them a stum-
bling-block to men who were ready enough
to use shibboleths as expressions of their
creed. Scarcely had Maurice found his foot-
hold in that large place, from which he never
was moved, before he was brought into contact with a church which appeared to be
breaking up into schools and parties, and
with a society which was avowedly atheistic,
as well as one more dangerously pharisaic.
These conditions never shook his faith in
unity, and his prophetic function was to declare a church and a nation which were wit-
nesses to God. " If ever I do any good
work," he writes, " and earn any of the
hatred which the godly in Christ Jesus received and have a right to, it must be in the
way I have indicated : by proclaiming society and humanity to be divine realities *as
they stand*, not as they may become, and by
calling upon the priests, kings, prophets of
the world to answer for their sin in having
made them unreal by separating them from
the living and eternal God, who has estab-

lished them in Christ for His glory. This is
what I call digging ; this is what I oppose
to building. And the more I read the Epis-
tle to the Corinthians, the more I am con-
vinced that this was St. Paul's work, the
one by which he hoped to undermine and to
unite the members of the Apollos, Cephas,
Pauline, and Christian (for those who said,
'We are of Christ' were the worst canters
and dividers of all) schools. Christ the actual foundation of the universe, not Christ
a Messiah to those who received him and
shaped him according to some notion of
theirs ; the head of a body, not the teacher
of a religion, was the Christ of St. Paul.
And such a Christ I desire to preach, and
to live in, and die in."

It is not surprising that Maurice, attempt-
ing, in his happy phrase, to undermine and
unite all parties, found himself outside of
all and attacked by all. He would not have
been a prophet if he had not been driven
into the wilderness more than once. That
did not stop his prophesying, and every time
that he was thus expelled multitudes followed him. His biographer, in speaking of
the burst of recognition which Maurice's
services received after his death, says, " It

was said to me, by more than one man, at
the time, that the spontaneity and universal-
ity of the feeling was so marked that there
did not seem to them to have been anything
like it in England since the Duke of Wel-
lington's death." Similar outbursts came
during Maurice's life-time, — on the occasion of his expulsion from his theological
professorship in King's College, for example ; but for the most part he was misrep-
resented and reviled by the religious press.
For it was against the bitter exclusiveness
and arrogance which found their worst expression in these journals that Maurice
waged an untiring warfare. The truth
which he maintained was sharper than a
two-edged sword, and made many divisions.
He would not have been a prophet, again,
if he had not possessed a fiery indignation
against all who shut up God in any one of
the cages of human insolence, or who would
make traffic of divine things. Colonel Maurice cites a striking instance of this indignation. His father was present at a club
when the question under discussion was the
subscription of the clergy.

"In the course of it a member of Parlia-
ment, a strict adherent of the religion of the

hour, had been emphatically insisting upon the necessity of tightly tying down the clergy to their belief in the current dogmas of the day, and of his particular school ; assuming throughout that just the creed of him and his friends was that which had always and everywhere been held by all. Pointing out the shocks which this form of faith had been of late receiving from many quarters, and suggesting a doubt whether the clergy were really giving their money's worth of subserviency for the money paid to them, he had said, ' Sometimes one would like to know what the clergy do believe nowadays ! '

" Every sentence had added fuel to the passionate indignation with which my father listened. It seemed to him just that claim to bind the clergy at the chariot wheels of public opinion against which he believed that the creeds, the articles, the fixed stipends of the clergy, the order of bishops as fathers in God, were so mary protests. It seemed just that convenient getting rid of all belief in a living God, and safely disposing of Him under a series of propositions, to be repeated at so much an hour, which he looked upon as the denial of the day.

His growing excitement became so manifest that a note was passed up to Mr. Kempe by one of those sitting by, begging Mr. Kempe to call next on Mr. Maurice. My father rose, as all those who saw him say, ' on fire.' ' Mr. —— asks what the clergy believe in nowadays. I believe in God the Father Almighty,' continuing the Apostles' Creed. Then he went on passionately to declare that because he so believed he was bound by his orders to protest against all appeals to money, to the praise of men, to the bargaining of the market, to the current run of popular feeling, as so many direct denials of truth, so many attempts to set up idols in place of the teaching of the living God. From all sides I have heard men say that it was one of the most striking things they had ever witnessed. Every one felt as if the place was in a blaze. No one else felt in any condition to speak, and the discussion abruptly ended."

" There were times," says his biographer elsewhere, " when he could make his words sting like a lash and burn like a hot iron. The very nature of his appeal, always to a man's own conscience, to his sense of right within the scope in which the man himself clearly discerned what was right and what was wrong, the full recognition of ability when he complained that it was being abused, the utter absence of any desire to dictate in details or to require any conformity to his own opinions, seemed, as it were, when he spoke indignantly, to carry the man addressed, then and there, 'unhousel'd, disappointed, unanel'd,' before the tribunal with which rests 'the ultimate and highest decision upon men's deeds, to which all the unjustly condemned at human tribunals appeal, and which weighs not the deed only, but motives, temptations, and ignorances, and all the complex conditions of the deed.' There were some to whom he so spoke who never forgave him. The marvelous thing, considering the depth to which he sometimes cut, is that there were so few.

" Whenever something that he looked upon as morally wrong or mean excited his wrath, he began in a most violent manner to rub together the palms of his two hands. The fits of doing so would often come on quite suddenly, as a result of his reflections on some action, as frequently as not of the religious world, or of so-called religious people. He appeared at such moments to be

entirely absorbed in his own reflections, and
utterly unconscious of the terrible effect
which the fierce look of his face and the
wild rubbing of his hands produced upon
an innocent bystander. A lady, who often
saw him thus, says that she always expected
sparks to fly from his hands, and to see him
bodily on fire. Certainly the effect was very
tremendous, and by no means pleasant."

This indignation appears more than once
in Maurice's correspondence, but the pre-
vailing impression upon the reader's mind
is rather of the singular charity which he
showed to all men, by virtue of which he
frequently disconcerted those who were in
opposition to him. For he would accept
what his opponent said, place himself on the
same side, and begin to argue the whole
matter from a stand-point apparently inim-
ical to himself. An amusing story of his
gentleness and of his determination to recognize the good is told apropos of his inability to manage a number of wild colts in
the lecture room of King's College. A boy
was disturbing the lecture. Maurice looked
up, and after watching him for a few moments said, "I do not know why that gentleman is doing what he is, but I am sure it

is for some great and wise purpose ; and if
he will come here and explain to us all what
it is, we shall be delighted to hear him."
This shows a habit of mind which even in
sarcasm falls into its natural form of speech.

The actual contribution which Maurice
made to the development of philosophic or
theologic thought does not consist in any
treatise which may serve as an armory for
polemic uses. The great power which he
exercised over the minds of men was in his
varied application of a few simple, profound
truths. His distinction, for example, of the
idea of eternal from that of everlasting,
while not original with him, was in his
hands a candle with which he lighted many
dark passages. His controversy with Mansel showed him inferior to his antagonist in
logical fence ; but what with Mansel was a
philosophic position was with Maurice a ter-
ribly practical truth, and he was constantly
expressing it, not in terms of philosophy,
but in terms of history, politics, and ethics.
It was the illuminating power of truth which
Maurice knew how to use. Many a student
of his writings has gone to them for an exegesis of some passage of the Bible, and
come away with a revelation which put to

A MODERN PROPHET 93

shame his small measures of textual truth. It is a favorite advice of commentators, Study the context; but Maurice's context was likely enough a piece of current English history, or an extract from Plato. No theologian of recent days has so broken down middle walls of partition in the minds of men.

It has rarely been given to men to see a few large truths so vividly as Maurice saw them, and at the same time to apply them to conduct and study with such vehement energy. Nevertheless, the very width of his vision may have led him to overlook a very present and near truth. In his anxiety to divest the idea of eternity of any time element, he missed, I think, that instinctive, or if not instinctive, then highly educated, conception of another world as a future world. He was right when he called back men from the postponement of moral consequences to a consideration of them in their essential properties, but he made too little of that reinforcement of the idea of eternity which comes through the sense of futurity. That sense is so imbedded in the consciousness as to revolt at last against the exclusive terms of Maurice's definitions. After all,

the predictive function of the prophet belongs to him, even if it be subordinate, and
that Maurice should have disregarded its
operation in his own case is all the more
singular, since hope was so emphatically the
key-note of his gospel.

LANDOR AS A CLASSIC.

Do readers, nowadays, resort to Landor's *Imaginary Conversations?* Writers of English respect the work so highly that it is a rare thing for any one to attempt to imitate Landor in this form of composition. He invented a variation of literary form, and was so consummate a master in it that it is almost as if he had taken out a patent which cautious authors feared to infringe. Readers thus have a peculiar possession in the work, though I suspect that it is writers chiefly who have recourse to Landor, — that he is a literary man's author, as others have been poets of poets.

The general reader who does not treat himself severely in the matter of reading may be expected to pass by some of the more recondite subjects and to rest at those volumes which contain the *Dialogues of Literary Men and Famous Women,* and the *Miscellaneous Dialogues.* For while all the dialogues presuppose a knowledge of history and literature, the actors in these are most familiar to the reader, and the topics discussed are neither so obscure nor so remote from common interest as are those presented in the other volumes. Not that Landor is ever exclusive in his interests ; it is the very reach of his sympathy which makes some of his dialogues more unreadable than others, for there are few humiliations to the ingenuous reader of modern English literature deeper than that which awaits him when he tries to follow the lead of this remarkable writer, who passes without the sign of toil from converse with ancients to talk with moderns, and seems capable of displaying a wonderful puppet-show of all history.

Perhaps the rank respectfully but without enthusiasm accorded to Landor is due mainly to the exactions which he makes of the reader. There must be omniscient readers for such an omniscient writer, and it cannot be denied that the ordinary reader takes his enjoyment of Landor with a certain stiffening of his faculties ; he feels it impossible to read him lazily. The case is not very unlike that of a listener to music, who has not a musical education and has an honest delight in a difficult work, while yet perfectly aware that he is missing, through his lack of technical knowledge, some of the finest expression. With classical works as with music, one commonly prefers to read what he has read before. Hamlet to the occasional reader of Shakespeare is like the Fifth Symphony to the occasional hearer of Beethoven. To ask him to read Landor is to ask him to hear Kalkbrenner, requiring him to form new judgments upon the old standard.

The pleasure which awaits the trained reader, on taking up Landor, is very great. At first there is the breadth and sweetness of the style. To come upon it after the negligence, the awkwardness, or the cheap brilliancy of much that passes for good writing, is to feel that one has entered the society of one's intellectual superiors. One might almost expect, upon discovering how hard Landor rode his hobby of linguistic reform, to find conceits and archaisms, or fantastic experiments in language; but as it was Landor's respect for sound words which lay at the bottom of his inconsistent attempts to remove other inconsistencies, the same respect forbade him to use the English language as if it were an individual possession of his own. Neither can it be said that his famil-

iarity with Latin forms misled him into sol-
ecisms in English; here, again, the very
perfection of his classical skill was turned to
account in rendering his use of English the
masterly employment of one of the dialects
of all language. Yet, though there is no
pedantry of a scholar perceptible in the English style, the phrase falls upon the ear
almost as a translation. It is idiomatic English, yet seems to have a relation to other
languages. This is partly to be referred to
the subjects of many of the dialogues, partly
to the dignity and scholarly tone of the work,
but is mainly the result of the cast of mind
in Landor, which was eminently classic,
freed, that is, from enslaving accidents, yet
always using with perfect fitness the characteristics which seem at a near glance to be
merely accidents. This is well illustrated by
those dialogues which are placed in periods
strongly individualized, as the Elizabethan
and the Puritan, or present speakers whose
tone is easily caught when overheard. A
weaker writer would, for example, mimic
Johnson in the conversations which occur
between him and Horne Tooke; Landor
catches Johnson's tone without tickling the
ear with idle sonorous phrases. A writer

who had read the dramatists freely, and set
out to represent them in dialogue, would be
very likely to use mere tricks of speech,
but Landor carefully avoids all stucco orna-
mentation, and makes the reader sure that
he has overheard the very men themselves.
It was the pride of Landor's design not to
insert in any one of his conversations " a
single sentence written by or recorded of
the personages who are supposed to hold
them." In the conversation between Lord
Brooke and Sir Philip Sidney, he makes
Sidney say, " To write as the ancients have
written, without borrowing a thought or expression from them, is the most difficult
thing we can achieve in poetry ; " and the
task which Landor set himself was an infinitely higher and finer one than the merely
ingenious construction of a closely joined
mosaic. He has extended the lives of the
men and women who appear in his dialogues.

The faithfulness with which Landor has
reproduced the voices of his characters follows from the truthfulness of the characters,
as they betray their natures in these conversations. This I have already intimated, and
it is the discovery of the reader who pene-
trates the scenes and is able in any case to

compare the men and women of Landor with
the same as they stand revealed in history
or literature. The impersonations are necessarily outlined in conversation. Revelation
through action is not granted, except occasionally in some such delicate form as hinted in
the charming scene between Walton, Cotton,
and Oldways. These delicate hints of action
will sometimes escape the reader through
their subtlety, but they tell upon the art of
the conversations very strongly. Still, the
labor of disclosing character is borne by the
dialogue, and success won in this field is of
the highest order. No one who uses conversation freely in novel-writing, when the talk
is not to advance the incidents of the story,
but to fix the traits of character held by the
persons, can fail to perceive Landor's remarkable power. He deals, it is true, with
characters already somewhat definitely existing in the minds of his intelligent readers,
yet he gives himself no advantage of a setting for his conversation, by which one might
make place, circumstance, scenery, auxiliary
to the interchange of sentiment and opinion.
Perhaps the most perfect example of a conversation instinct with meaning, and permit-
ting, one may say, an indefinite column of

foot-notes, is the brief, exquisitely modulated one between Henry VIII. and Anne Boleyn.

It may be that we have received the best good to be had from literature when we have been enabled to perceive men and women brightly, and to hold for a time before our eyes those who once were seen by persons more blessed only than we. Certain it is that to the solitary student, placed, it may be, in untoward circumstance, such a gift is priceless. But it belongs with this as a necessary accompaniment, if not a further good, to have such a discovery of character as comes through high thought and wise sentiment. The persons whom Landor has vivified have burst their cerements for no mean purpose. They are summoned, not for idle chit-chat, but to speak words befitting them in their best moments. Southey is said to have remarked on the conversation which he is made to hold with Porson, that they might not have conversed as Landor had shown them, " but we could neither of us have talked better." It is Landor's power not only to inhabit the characters, but to inhabit them worthily, that makes these books great. The subjects discussed are such as great-minded men might discuss, and it is when one marks the range of topics and the height to which the thought rises that he perceives in Landor a moralist as well as a dramatist. It is true that the judgments and opinions which he puts into the mouths of speakers partake of his own wayward, impetuous nature, and it would not be hard to find cases where the characters clearly Landorize, but the errors are in noble not in petty concerns.

There is, doubtless, something of labor in reading Landor's *Conversations* if one is not conversant with high thinking, and if one is but slenderly endowed with the historic imagination, but the labor is not in the writing. The very form of conversation permits a quickness of transition and sudden shifting of subject and scene which enliven the art and give an inexhaustible variety of light and shade. One returns to passages again and again for their exceeding beauty of expression and their exquisite setting. To one accustomed to the glitter of current epigrammatic writing, the brilliancy of some of Landor's sentences may not at first be counted for its real worth, but to go from Landor to smart writers is to exchange jewels for paste.

What I have said may serve partly to explain the limited audience which Landor has had and must continue to have. If it is a liberal education to read his writings, it requires one to receive them freely. The appeal which Landor makes to the literary class is very strong, and apart from a course of study in the Greek and Latin classics, I doubt if any single study would serve an author so well as the study of Landor. Indeed, there is perhaps no modern work which gives to the reader not familiar with Greek or Latin so good an idea of what we call classical literature. Better than a translation is the original writing of Landor for conveying the aroma which a translation so easily loses. The dignity of the classics, the formality, the fine use of sarcasm, the consciousness of an art in literature, — all these are to be found in the *Imaginary Conversations;* and if a reader used to the highly seasoned literature of recent times complains that there is rather an absence of humor, and that he finds Landor sometimes dull, why, Heaven knows we do not often get hilarious over our ancient authors, and Landor, for his contemporaries, is an ancient author with a very fiery soul.

A survey of all his work increases the

admiration, not unmixed with fear, with which one contemplates the range of this extraordinary writer. The greatest of his dialogues are great indeed, but the facility with which he used this form betrayed him into employing it for the venting of mere vagaries, and the prolix discussion of topics of contemporary politics and history, by no means of general interest. Still, after all deductions are made, the work as a whole remains great, and I repeat that a study of Landor would be of signal service to any faithful man of letters. In his style he would discover a strength and purity which would constantly rebuke his own tendencies to verbosity and unmeaning phrases; in the respect which Landor had for great writers he would learn the contemptible character of current irreverence in literature ; in the sustained flight of Landor's thought he would find a stimulus for his own less resolute nature ; and as Landor was himself no imitator, so the student of Landor would discover how impossible it was to imitate him, how much more positive was the lesson to make himself a master by an unceasing reverence of masters and a fearless independence of inferiors. Landor is sometimes character-

ized as arrogant and conceited ; stray words
and acts might easily be cited in support of
this, but no one can read his *Conversations*
intelligently and not perceive how noble was
his scorn of mean men, how steadfast his
admiration of great men.

DR. MUHLENBERG.

A BELIEF in Apostolic Succession does
not preclude one from an independent belief
in the continual appearance, even if in broken succession, of apostles whose credentials
are to be found in their apostolic life. It
has seemed to some that Dr. Muhlenberg
was a man born out of due time, and that
there was an anachronism in his flourishing
in the nineteenth century. Both his familiar
friends and strangers were wont to remark
on a certain likeness in character and presence to S. John the Divine, and the repetition by him in varying forms of that doctrine
of Christian brotherhood which is so emphatically announced in the older apostle's
letters and gospel has made the comparison
a natural one; yet no one can read Dr. Muhlenberg's *Life*, as written by Sister Anne,
and regard him as in any sense presenting
an extinct or antiquated type of Christianity.
The picturesqueness, so to speak, of his life,
which has struck people so forcibly, had not

a particle of unreality about it : there was
no assumption of some obsolete phase of
religious manners, nor was there any masquerading in devotion ; the genuineness of
his nature was utterly opposed to anything
of this sort, but there was in him a poetic
sensibility which led him to appropriate
whatever was native to him in historic Christianity, and a poetic power which found
expression less in verse than in a certain
unique and very beautiful effort after the
restoration of order in human life. He was a
religious poet : but though his name in literature is joined to one or two musical hymns,
the true place to look for his art is in the
memorial movement, in the cluster of char-
ities of which the Church of the Holy Communion and S. Luke's Hospital are the
centres, and in St. Johnland. In the inception of these projects he showed the artist's
power, as in their conception he had showed
a poet's insight, and both the conceiving and
the realization were marked by a genuine
religious faith.

It is the merit of this delightful biography
that, while it is written with no singular
skill, it is unusually transparent as a medium through which to reward a remarkable

man.   There are no marks of suppression
by the biographer; apparently her single aim
was to clear away whatever might withdraw
attention from her subject, and the book
thus leads the reader on to the close with an
unflagging interest.   It is rare indeed to
find so unpretending and so successful a
piece of biographic work.   There was everything in the subject to tempt an ambitious
writer into making a fine portrait; as I
have intimated, the character is so unique
and its expression so original that it would
have been easy to throw an air of improba-
bility over the whole by emphasizing certain
characteristics.   As it is, the truthfulness of
the picture is warranted by the unaffected-
ness with which it is painted.

It was Dr. Muhlenberg's fortune to be
easily misunderstood.   At a time when the
church to which he belonged was timid and
suspected, he used its liturgical stores with a
freedom and an effectiveness which startled
his associates, and upon the appearance of
the Tractarian movement in the Church of
England he was quickly identified with it in
the minds of those who judged exclusively
from a use of symbols and forms common to
him and the English ritualists.   He was

himself attracted by the revival in England of ecclesiastical æsthetics, and for a moment seemed ready to be drawn into the deeper currents of the stream ; but a resolute examination of the ground on which he stood was followed by a more positive assertion of his acceptance of what is known as the evangelical creed. The simple courage and sincerity of the man were displayed in his refusal to abandon practices and forms which he held to be historical in the church, and not the exclusive property of the new party, although associated with the doctrines of that party in most people's minds. Thus he was looked upon with suspicion both by the sacerdotalists and the evangelicals. It was not that he steered a middle course between these extremes, but that in a perfectly modest and unobtrusive manner he asserted his independence, and gave free expression to his belief and his poetic nature.

He was imagined by many also to be an unpractical enthusiast. The real truth was that Dr. Muhlenberg not only believed in the ideal which his generous and poetic nature perceived, but he regarded it as something to be made real, something of larger worth than dreams, and he had the patience and perseverance which put more practical men to shame. It was his magnificent faith which thus built S. Luke's Hospital and made it a real Hôtel Dieu, and the picture which is given of his own residence there and paternal charge is exquisitely beautiful. So his latest, and we think his noblest, dream of St. Johnland was precisely one of those poetic fancies which have stirred men to hopes and aspirations, but furnished him with a solid scheme to be labored over and achieved. A village expressing Christian socialism in definite outline was the result, and while the *Life* does not furnish us with all the details which we could wish of this very interesting experiment, enough is displayed to make the picture of the founder upon his eightieth birthday something more than the graceful sketch of a king in no-man's land. An endowment fund of twenty thousand dollars had been raised in connection with St Johnland, and it was desired to make it known to him on that birthday : —

"He was induced to make the journey the evening before, so that he might be rested for the demands of the morrow. He rose bright and well the next morning at an early hour, and the first event of the day

was his acceptance, while yet in his chamber,
of this grateful tribute. He was left alone
with his emotions for a while; then a choir
of voices broke out in song on the green-
sward northward of the house. Young and
old had gathered below his windows at break
of day, to wish him joy of his eighty years,
in the native birthday lyric sacred to his
anniversary. He threw up the sash and
looked out. It was a beautiful sight. Every
upturned face, standing a little aslant that
they might see him the better, was illu-
mined by the newly risen sun, and beaming
also with the pleasure of his presence.
Leaning forward a little, that he might take
in the whole, his countenance irradiated
with holy love and his arms stretched out
and over them in unspoken benediction, he
stood there awaiting the termination of their
singing. Scarcely had the last word died
upon their lips, when his own voice, strong
and sonorous, led them in ' Praise God from
whom all blessings flow.' Then came the
Lord's Prayer in heartiest accord, followed
by a fervent, soul - breathing benediction,
after which they dispersed for breakfast in
the several families, and every household
later had a brief, sweet visit from him. . . .

In the afternoon came the ordinary festiv-
ities of the founder's birthday for the whole
settlement, in the fine old grove. It was
thought that the previous exertions of the
day would make him unable to be among
his children there; but in the midst of their
hilarity, some one joyfully exclaimed, ' Why,
there's Dr. Muhlenberg!' He had walked
up alone from the house, and was pausing a
moment on the brow of the hill to gaze upon
the scene. His slender form stood out
strongly against the golden autumnal sky,
the soft, rich hues of which were all in
harmony with the ripe saintliness of his
well-nigh perfected spirit. He joined the
holiday-makers, and all went as merrily as if
that were not the last time he and his St.
Johnlanders would ever be together again
upon earth."

The institutions which he called into life
may have a longer or shorter existence:
they were built to endure, and they include
principles which are no mere idle vagaries
of an enthusiast; but the longest life possible to them can hardly add to the testimony
which his character and ambition receive
from them. The humility of the man, his
unfeigned desire to serve, his ardent temper-

ament husbanding all resources for positive
beneficence, and his nature freely giving of
its own abundance through channels only
dreamed of by others, — these have a per-
ennial charm. And of how much greater
worth to the Church is a man than an insti-
tution! There is, of course, a certain absurdity in the comparison, yet we are unconsciously given to elevating institutions as
if they held, by virtue of their organization,
an originating power; and we are liable to
be put out in our calculations by men and
women, especially if they are endowed with
genius. We are tempted to classify men,
and then to refer results or movements to
the party which seems to be the moving
cause; but, after all, we are obliged to remember that not parties, but persons, constitute the Church. With what singular force
the character and work of Dr. Muhlenberg
recall us to the living power of a devoted,
consecrated saint. I am not afraid to use
the word of him; he helps us to bring back
the term to its apostolic significance, and to
think of it, not as indicating a better man
than the common run of men, but one set
apart for divine service. Here was a saint
who served, and the very originality of his

service makes his character more powerful as an example. For the stimulus is, not to attempt the work which one feels was impossible to be copied, but to live the consecrated life which is as varied in its expression as humanity itself. Dr. Muhlenberg was a poet whose best lines were in the stones of the Church of the Holy Communion, the bricks of S. Luke's Hospital, and the broad acres of St. Johnland. That poetry was the work of genius, but the consecration of the poet is the hope and not the despair of men.

AMERICAN HISTORY ON THE STAGE.

PUBLIC taste in America has of late years taken two lines that have a tendency to converge into one, and I have been watching curiously to see what the result would be. Every one has observed the marked increase of interest in American history. The impetus was given by the anniversaries which clustered about the opening of a second century in national life. At these anniversaries great oratorical exhibitions were given, where men and women assisted with attention and applause ; lectures, books, magazine articles, and public gatherings of various sorts attested the interest. The newspapers, reflecting the popular taste, gave an amount of space to historical subjects which would have buried them in bankruptcy if it had not been that the readers of newspapers wanted all that was given them.

Not only this, but a vigorous effort has been made to reconstruct to the eye the historic past. We have had exhibitions of historical curiosities, and a lively competition has been set up for the possession of historical bric-a-brac. Even our houses have rapidly acquired an historic imposture. People have put on their ancestors' clothes, and have tried by games, theatricals, tableaux, and masquerades to see how the heroes looked who have suddenly come forward in such near perspective. There is something almost pathetic in the eagerness with which, but a few years ago, everybody was centennializing himself, and looking over his shoulder to catch a glimpse of the century behind him in the mirror which he held. How charmingly the young American girl slipped into the Revolutionary costume! the only one of us, I am sure, who really reproduced the past. Howells caught her at her gentle masquerading, and drew her portrait in his sonnet to Dorothy Dudley, the feigned chronicler of the Cambridge of 1776 : —

" Fair maiden, whom a hundred summers keep
    Forever seventeen, and whose dark locks
    Are whitened only from the powder-box,
After these many winters : on the steep
Of high-heeled shoes, and with the silken sweep
    Of quaint brocade, and an arch smile that mocks
    At Time's despite, thy lovely semblance walks.

This year, our continent from deep to deep,
    At numberless Centennial Tea-Parties,
    With chicken-salad, coffee, chocolate
For retrospective youth, whose bosoms swell,
    When they behold thee and thy pleasing freight,
    With love of country, and each patriot sees
Thy charm in all that thou dost chronicle."

Now the interest in this amiable masquerade is part also of the new taste in theatricals. It would be quite as easy to show that the period which witnessed the Centennial fever saw also a great increase in dramatic entertainments of an amateur character. The theatre has its own history and development, dependent upon conditions often only remotely connected with other phases of social life; and it does not follow, because there has been an extraordinary impulse given to private theatricals, that there has also been a corresponding popular interest in the regular stage. Yet there is a connection between the two. Amateur theatricals educate audiences rather than actors. Now and then a person discovers a talent for acting by taking part in amateur performances, but it cannot be said that such performances are in any way a school for the stage. What we are justified in inferring is, that the increased activity in private dramatic enter-

tainments points to a wider interest in the
drama, a greater familiarity with plays, and
an accession to the ranks of theatre-goers
from a part of the community not hitherto
especially given to frequenting the theatre.

Generalizing on such a subject is usually
only the writer's private impressions, so my
assertion may be taken for what it is worth,
that the readers of good literature have not,
as a rule, in America, been supporters of the
theatre, but that in this class there has
sprung up of late a decided interest in the
drama, and that this interest is to affect the
stage.   The adhesion of the literary class
— both the writers and the readers of books
— to the drama, which has gradually come
about, is likely to cause a different order of
plays, and in various respects to modify the
present state of things.

It must be remembered that Puritanism
and literature combined have caused the
theatre in England, and still more in America, to hold a position which is not necessarily permanent.   That is, the theatre has
been made more exclusively a place of
amusement than it has been in France, Italy,
or Germany.   The drama has been so far
divorced from literature that we have been

taught to make a distinction between plays
to be acted and plays to be read, — a distinction almost as irrational as songs to be
recited and songs to be sung. Each has
gone its own way and formed its own tradition. The drama, thrown in upon itself, has
been developed independently of literary
influences. It has come to rely largely on
stage effects ; that is, it has used the material at its disposal with reference to points
of display, and has subordinated the text of
the play to the actors, the scenery, and the
dresses. It has turned novels which were
dramatic into plays which excite the ridicule
of the critics who praised the novels, and it
has been dependent for its new blood either
on translations or on dramatic artisanship,
neither of which contains any real inspiration. It has allied itself with business
rather than with letters, and a strong tendency has been shown toward the merely
spectacular.

On the other hand, literature, for lack of
this healthful outlet, has been driven within
narrower bounds ; has contracted its power,
lost a fine faculty of expression, and tended
to insulate society instead of making it
mobile. Society, when intellectually occu-

pied, might almost be pictured as a household sitting in the evening around a table, with backs to the light, for the sake of saving weak eyes, each reading to himself, "all silent," as Shelley says, —

" All silent and all damned."

Shut out from the stage, literature has tried to make itself vivid through other forms. The novel, in the hands of Dickens and his school, was distinctly affected by the effort to introduce stage effects by merely mental processes ; and it is largely owing to the same cause that literature has developed a farcical quality of humor, — the painful effort of a book to do what a comedian does easily with a contortion of face.

Now, in the popular awakening to the worth of American history, in the new interest felt by educated people in the drama, may there not be discovered a restoration of old relations between literature and the stage, too long dissevered ? Such a combination of literary and dramatic forces must depend for permanence upon the audience, and it is the audience which has been in process of education. The principal facts and personages in American history are

every year becoming more positively a part
of the furniture of the average mind, and
there is a more familiar acquaintance with
what may be called the scenery and properties of history through the aid of museums,
collections, exhibitions, pictures, and picture-
books. It is from this common acquaintance with history that any popular appreciation will come of literary work which is
based upon history. What is it in art that
makes subjects drawn from the Bible so
quickly received by the people, except that
familiarity with the book which renders it
unnecessary for the artist to add a literary
commentary to his picture? And when
American history is a household tale, then
we may look for a ready appreciation of literature suggested by it. The concentration
of attention, in manifold ways, upon this
subject, in schools and among young people
generally, is rapidly preparing the ground
for a literature which shall react upon the
subjects treated, and make history a still
more real and interesting thing to common
people. The rehabilitation of the stage
opens a conspicuous field for the exercise of
these forces.

Granting the possibility of a time, which

for my own pleasure I will make near at
hand, when author, audience, and actors
shall be ready, does our reading of American
history justify us in believing that it will be
a storehouse for dramatic incident and movement? Schlegel, in his *Lectures on Dramatic Art and Literature*, remarks that the
great requisite in the historical drama consists in this : " It must be a crowded extract
and a living development of history," — by
which I suppose him to mean that it shall
present a series of tableaux, which shall discover an actual growth and culmination of
historic life.   Now in the fullest and most
familiar portion of our early history, that of
New England, there are no tableaux, because
there are no groups and no contrasts appeal-
ing vividly to the eye.   The contrast which
we bear in mind is to the contemporary history of England, or the subsequent history
of America.   There is scarcely even a contrast of figures: the Indian makes the
sketchiest possible personage, and the Quaker, at this distance, is only another shade
of dun from the Puritan.   Then there is no
culmination of historic fact.   The history
has been called the march of a headless mob,
but there is not even the picturesque vio-

lence of a mob. We recognize the growth of ideas and the expansion of material prosperity, neither of which admits of very animated presentation; and there were no crises which could furnish corresponding dramatic points, — scarcely any persons of marked prominence for centres of dramatic interest.

Longfellow, with his unfailing perception of artistic values, seized upon the two tragic elements in early New England history, the persecution of the Quakers and the witchcraft delusion. These he significantly termed *The* New England Tragedies, and in arranging them he kept within historical bounds. If he did not expect them to be played, at least he took no advantage of the doubt to free himself from any restriction of the acted drama. Except that the scenes and acts are shorter than is common, nothing is lacking for a feasible representation on the boards, — but, one instinctively adds, on the boards of an amateur theatre. The high lights required on the regular stage would disclose the meagreness of the two plays as spectacles, while the possible refinement and delicacy of impersonation in an amateur performance, and the equalizing of text and setting, would disclose the grace and gentle charm of the situations. But any representation would be likely to show the inadequacy of the themes taken as historical pictures. When we bring Puritans and Quakers together in the little town of Boston, and take for the turning-point of the drama merely the expulsion of the Quakers, there is not enough appeal to the imagination to call out any very profound feeling. Moreover, there is no real culmination either in *John Endicott* or in *Giles Corey of the Salem Farms;* we are simply given scenes out of a very provincial history, with only remote reference to universal passions. It must be borne in mind that the poet viewed the themes as a part of his trilogy, and was occupied with their humanitarian aspect.

The persecution of the Quakers was simply an exhibition of the Puritan character and training; it sprang from nothing, it led to nothing; and spectacularly there is in the contrast of Puritan and Quaker only two shades of the same color, since modern decorum scarcely allows the Quaker to appear on the stage in his historic occasional dress. The witchcraft delusion does offer an opportunity for some passionate and fiery scenes; there is a chance for a lurid light against the sombre Puritan background, and for finely modeled figures in such persons as Sewall and Mather. A dramatic incident of value is to be found in the sudden revulsion of feeling which followed the indictment of Madam Hale as a witch ; that and Judge Sewall's confession would make telling points on the stage.

A better subject than either of these is to be found in the legend which Hawthorne used in *The Gray Champion*. A drama founded on Goffe's adventures would give a series of historic scenes in two continents, beginning with the trial of a king, and closing with an apparently miraculous interposition. It would have the great advantage of dealing with great subjects, and of introducing figures already familiar to the ordinary reader.

There is another subject in New England provincial history which offers dramatic situations, but it would perhaps be more correct to call it a passage in Canadian history ; and it has the misfortune of all Canadian subjects, that it suggests a tragedy without a fifth act. In 1690, Sir William Phips, at the head of an expedition of twenty-two hundred men,— shipmasters, merchants, master mechanics, and substantial farmers, — sailed out of Boston harbor to attack and capture Quebec. Phips's own history is one of romantic interest, and this bluff, choleric, prompt, rude man stands opposed to the picturesque governor of Canada, Count Frontenac, one of that long list of adventurous men who light the canvas of Canadian history with brilliant points. Frontenac sought the aid of the Indian in the defense of Quebec, and a grand council of all the tribes of the lakes was held. At this council a curious scene occurred, which I give in Mr. Parkman's words : —

" Frontenac [at this time a man of seventy] took a hatchet, brandished it in the air, and sang the war song. The principal Frenchmen present followed his example. The Christian Iroquois of the two neighboring missions joined them, and so also did the Hurons and Algonquins of Lake Nipissing, stamping and screeching like a troop of madmen, while the governor led the dance, whooping like the rest. His predecessor would have perished rather than play such a part in such a company, but the punctilious old courtier was himself half an Indian at heart, — as much at home in a wigwam as in the halls of princes."

The actual fighting before Quebec was insignificant. Phips waited for reinforcements, and kept up only a feeble cannonading. Meanwhile, he tried the effect of a summons to surrender, and his messenger, received blindfold into the town, was conducted by tortuous ways, and amid the jeers of the populace, to the château, where, when the bandage was removed, his eye dropped before the haughty presence of Frontenac, surrounded by French and Canadian officers, glittering with all the gay insignia of rank and office. The interview was short and contemptuous; the New England general was bluffed by the Frenchman, and withdrew from the contest just as he was about to be aided by a powerful ally, — famine. As he sailed away, "Quebec," says Parkman, "was divided between thanksgiving and rejoicing. The captured flag of Phips's ship was borne to the cathedral in triumph; the bishop sang *Te Deum;* and amid the firing of cannon the image of the Virgin was carried to each church and chapel in the place by a procession in which priest, people, and troops all took part. The day closed with a great bonfire in honor of Frontenac."

This historic event has the misfortune, as

I have intimated, of having been a failure
on Phips's part. It is necessary for us to be
on Frontenac's side to see the possibility of
a drama culminating in the triumph at the
withdrawal of Phips's fleet; and even then
we see how different for dramatic purposes
is a successful defense from a successful attack. What pleases me is the spectacular
element in the grouping of Frenchmen,
New Englanders, and Indians in Frontenac's breakdown and in the pageant. For
one, I like a good show on the stage, and I
commend this historic episode as offering a
capital background for a bright love story.

The career of Joseph Warren is not without dramatic hints. The Boston Massacre,
Warren's oration at the Old South, with his
suppression of the rumble of violence, and
his fall at Bunker Hill give points for representation of successive hours in the conflict
between Great Britain and America. For
the point of time was not only critical; it
held the larger development of the war in
miniature. And that is precisely what the
drama attempts; for the historical drama is
a microcosm, an epitome of the great conflict,
just as tragedy is an epitome of human life;
and when a single contest contains the germ

of an epoch, the dramatist has only to give it artistic selection. In the secret councils of the Committee of Safety, the arrogance and timidity of Governor Gage and the court party, the national instincts of the conscientious loyalists, the restlessness of the populace, the foresight and steadiness of a few patriots, we find the elements of true dramatic representation ; and it only needs to arrange these in a culminating series of events to give in reduced scale the entire historic movement.

Yet the Revolution, as we used to call it, is singularly lacking in dramatic properties. We are misled by the title ; the American Development would be a truer phrase, and it is observable that careful historical writers almost uniformly speak of the War for Independence. The French Revolution was rightly so called ; it shook to the centre an old order of things. The American Revolution set the seal to a foregone conclusion. It disturbed existing political relations, but not until new ones of a higher order were germinant. The very nature of the conflict interfered with strong dramatic situations, — situations, that is, which seem to hold soluble elements of national life for a moment, and suffer them to become indestructible before our eyes. There are romantic incidents, but the only group of events during the war which offers any opportunity for an historical drama is that relating to Arnold's treachery and André's execution. In those events there would be a chance to lift the figure of Washington into dramatic prominence.

We often hear it said, Happy the nation that has no history; but of course by that phrase is meant the nation that suffers no violence of war and devastation, for it is these things which, in the old conception of history, went to make up the account, — these and the quarrels of kings. In the more modern conception of history, which regards the movement of a nation toward the realization of freedom, there are many things besides war and quarrels which are reckoned; but it must be admitted that the possibilities of dramatic representation lie in circumstances of sharp change, and in the action of the passions. This is merely making use of the very etymon of the drama, which is a *thing done*, and done before our eyes. In the history of our country, when we leave behind the period of war, and the adjustment of parts which make the nation, what remains for representation in the historic drama? Plainly, not the progress of laws, nor the growth of cities, nor westward emigration, nor the finding of gold in California. The philosopher and economist and social novelist have the monopoly in such fields. Neither does the invention of the cotton-gin, the reaper, or the sewing-machine serve the purpose of the historical drama, though Mr. Whitman can cram them boldly into a lyric. They all help to make up our history, as do numberless other factors in civilization, but they are not dramatic in their nature.

It needs no special insight to see that the one subject which lies at the heart of our history since the Revolution is the one subject in which dramatic incidents are imbedded. Slavery and its extinction constitute the theme of our history since the Union was reached; and because the extinction of slavery has made possible a nation no longer divided by irreconcilable differences, there is always in every drama based on the slavery contest, however tragic may be its incidents, the possibility of a triumphant conclusion, accordant with history and the prophecy of history. The conflict for freedom is so large and so moving in its nature, and has always been so dramatic in its incident; its roots lie so deep in the moral nature, where alone the great drama thrives; and it is so involved in national development, that all other subjects in our history are weak and insignificant before the possibilities of this theme. We stand, perhaps, too near the scenes of the late war, and are too much a part of the conflict, to be able to bear the spectacle of that drama reënacted on the stage; but in due time the events not so much of the war as of the moral and political conflict will find adequate presentation, when the vast proportions of the theme will be reduced in epitome and made vivid in action, which concentrates the thought of the historic movement into a few characters and situations.

There is a subject — I had almost said the only subject — magnificently conspicuous, and capable of holding the entire history of American slavery and its downfall. The material for illustrating it is copious and well known; in parts, indeed, almost ready for use. It is just one of the cases where history pauses for a moment, puts its finger on the page, and says There! The immediate incidents and events, when compared with other scenes, look trivial; yet how perfectly typical and dramatic are every one of the facts which we possess regarding the life and death of Captain John Brown! Here is the moral indignation of the people finding expression in one sharp explosion ; here is the prophet saying, "Let my people go." Victor Hugo's sketch of John Brown on the gallows, which looks in the darkness like a cross, presents in a theatrical and offensive way the intense feeling which found in Brown a sacrifice for a great sin. The figure looms, in the midst of its fellows, into gigantic proportions. Even for those who call his character an insane and fanatic one his adventures have a strange fascination, and the farther we get away from the scenes the more typical do they become. The very smallness of the scale upon which his attempt at Harper's Ferry was made renders the action all the more fitted for dramatic copying, and none the less prefigurative of the mighty contest at hand; the failure of the attempt, moreover, holds a finer power than success.

The quaint Puritanic speech of the man

is singularly fitted to express the religious
and historical opposition to slavery. No
one can read the simple narrative of Brown's
conduct after his capture without perceiving
that history has furnished drama with the
very words he used, and almost the very order of those words. The conversation which
took place mainly between Mason, the author of the fugitive slave law, and Vallan-
digham on one side and John Brown on the
other is curiously dramatic in its character
and force. The letters of Brown and his
reported conversations are crowded with
characteristic, spontaneous expressions, so
that it would be entirely possible to present
the man in his own terms, and to find in
these truly poetical and fit language. Then
the incidents connected with his execution
are precisely of the kind to touch us with
their representative character : the taking
up of a negro child and caressing it ; the cry
of the old black woman, " God bless you,
old man ! I wish I could help you, but I
cannot ; " and it is a matter of tradition that
among the Virginia militia who surrounded
the gallows, and marched and counter-
marched, was Wilkes Booth.

These and other trivial incidents help to

show how rich in subsidiary action is the
entire dramatic scene. The great value of
it lies in its microcosmic presentation of the
mighty conflict so soon to shake the land.
The representatives of the slave power in
hotspur Governor Wise and the cold and
crafty Mason stood confronting Brown ; the
Northern apologist for slavery was there ;
and if it were necessary to confine the action
to Harper's Ferry, it would be quite possible
to bring upon the stage spokesmen for all
the leading parties in the country without
violating the facts of history.

A great drama is not to be had for the
ordering, any more than a great work of art
of any kind, but the chances for it are increased by the gradual recovery of the stage
to wider relations. The hope of good drama
does not lie in the repetition of old plays ; it
is not a dead power ; its life is in the present, and there can be no real vitality in the
drama in any country unless it takes root in
the soil. The drama is still a foreign thing
with us, — foreign from our traditional
tastes, and foreign in its appointments. To
my thinking the chance for greater things
lies through historic scenes rather than
through social contrasts. It is significant

that Tennyson, an Englishman through and through, expressed his political feeling in *Queen Mary*. It was not a success, because people are not yet accustomed to go to the theatre as they read the newspaper, and Tennyson shares in the disadvantage of taking up the drama as something foreign from English literary culture. His assumption of archaic forms of speech was an indication of his effort to bring his play into relation with the older English theatre; it suffered from its excess of antiquarianism. But Tennyson's failure points toward a change, and it is not impossible that in America, where prejudice sits more lightly on its throne, we may witness an increased consciousness of national being through the presentation of history in dramatic form, as well as through other forms of literary art, which have hitherto been more familiar to us. There has been gathering a delightful moss of legend and romance to cover the stony facts of our history. It may well be that the reader of Hawthorne and Irving and Whittier will yet have the pleasure of seeing the historic life of America epitomized on the stage in dramatic action.

THE SHAPING OF EXCELSIOR.

WHEN Hawthorne went through a virtuoso's collection he came upon Cornelius Agrippa's book of magic, in which were pressed many flowers; among these was Longfellow's *A Sprig of Fennel.* " It is as good, perhaps, as *Excelsior,*" writes Longfellow to Samuel Ward ; " Hawthorne, who is passing the night with me, likes it better." The title *Fennel* was changed, for the worse I think, to *The Goblet of Life.* That could not have been pressed in a book, to be sure, through the virtuoso might easily have had the goblet in some corner cupboard. But a visit to Harvard College Library gives one the opportunity to see a greater curiosity, — a bit of Longfellow's mind. Spread open in one of the cases are the first and second drafts of *Excelsior*, and a rare chance is given of seeing how a poet, when he has seized upon the central thought of a poem, will sometimes work industriously at its final form.

The first draft was written upon the blank spaces of a letter received by the poet from Charles Sumner, so that the very paper of the poem had already an historic interest. If it were worth while one might stop a moment to note the appositeness of the material, since Sumner had in him very much of the spirit of the aspiring young man, when he wrote his note to Longfellow, and was just the person to have carried the banner if he had happened to think of that mode of expression. The first stanza, with its erasures, is as follows : —

> The shades of night were falling fast
>
> When through an Alpine village pass'd
>   ~~through~~ snow and ice
>   bore ~~above all price~~
>   'mid
> A youth who ~~as the peasant sung~~
>
> A banner with the strange device
>
> ~~Responded in an unknown tongue,~~
>
>   *Excelsior !*

The poet's first attempt was at a contrasted image of the peasant's humble life with its contentment, and the aspiration of the youth unintelligible to the peasant in the valley. It was too soon to introduce this contrast; he resolved to show the youth only, not speaking, but silently displaying his symbol, precious however to himself. Then the preciousness appeared commonplace or necessarily involved in the very action of the youth, and the poet returned to the idea of a contrast, but this time a contrast of cold, indifferent nature and passionate, spiritual man. What an immense advance in fullness of expression ! It is curious, however, that in the second draft, on another paper, also preserved, the poet returned to this idea and tried again, —

A youth who bore a pearl of price, —

possibly seeking to connect the image with the Biblical one in order to suggest the interpretation of his parable by linking it with an accepted image of spiritual contempt of the world. There is a slight verbal correction also in *'mid* for *through*, as if the physical difficulty of *through ice* annoyed him. The second stanza in the first draft reads : —

his eye beneath

His brow was sad ; ~~but underneath~~

Flash'd like a faulchion from its sheath

~~His steel blue eye~~

rung
And like a silver clarion ~~sung,~~
The accents of that
~~His sweet voice~~ in an unknown tongue,

Excelsior !

Here he was dissatisfied as soon as he had
half completed the third line, for he had finished the idea and had half a line to spare.
He went back, struck out *but underneath*,
wrote *his eye beneath*, which instantly gave
him the compactness he wished and a
straightforwardness of construction also.
Then, probably, when he had said that his
sweet voice sung like a silver clarion, he reflected that a clarion rung rather than sung,
and changing this word, he saw that in the
accents of the tongue he had a more ringing
power than he had in a sweet voice, and certainly not only is the measure of the last
line now better, but there has been a great
access of virility; the mere change of *sung*
to *rung* has lifted the third line into something like a trumpet-note.

In the third stanza, the first draft showed
only two slight alterations; in the first line
he wrote *humble homes,* which he changed
to *happy homes*, thus presenting a stronger
contrast to the youth's loneliness, and in

the second he changed *pure and bright* to *clear and bright*, but the whole stanza was unsatisfactory as it then stood:

> In happy homes he saw the light
>
> Of household fires gleam clear and bright,
>
> And far o'erhead the glaciers shone,
>
> His lips breath'd with a stifled groan,
>
> *Excelsior !*

The labor appears in the second draft, where the first two lines are the same, but the second two are thus worked over: —

> Above the spectral
> ~~And far above~~ the glaciers shone;
> And from his lips escaped a
> ~~His lips repress'd the rising~~ groan.

Not only is the rhythm better in this last line, but the action is far more poetic, while both lines have gained in nervous force and in their connection with each other. As first written, there was an awkward halt at the close of the third line. In the final revision one other change was introduced by making the fires gleam *warm and bright* instead of *clear and bright*, which was a weak redundancy, while warm also intensifies the contrast.

The fourth stanza came easily. The first three lines were unchanged in the first draft or the second, and stood as they do in the printed form. The fourth line in the first draft appeared

his clarion
And clear ~~that youthful~~ voice replied ;

in the second draft, it was

loud
And ~~clear~~ his clarion voice replied ;

in the poem it now reads

And loud that clarion voice replied.

Slight changes these, but in the direction of euphony and picturesqueness. It may be said that *youthful* in its contrast to the *old man* was preferable, but it was not so euphonic, and *clarion*, though used before, was probably taken as suggesting, with loudness, the spiritual cry of the young man heard above the physical voice of the tempest and torrent.

There is some uncertainty in deciphering the erasures of the fifth stanza. In the corrections, however, there is no singular variation of form except that in the third line, *pale blue eye* became altered to *bright blue eye ;* possibly the poet at first meant to indi-

cate his weariness by *pale*, and then resolved
to give rather his resolution in *bright*.

In the sixth stanza *the pine tree's withered branch* is an improvement upon the
first form, which appeared in both drafts,
the withered pine tree's branch and *awful
avalanche* was first the tamer *falling avalanche*.

The seventh stanza was wholly rewritten,
and recast. Besides the linear erasures,
lines are drawn downward, marking out the
whole, and a new stanza takes its place.

> And as the
> ~~The pious~~ monks of Saint Bernard
>
> In haste the convent gate unbarr'd
> They
> ~~And~~ heard amid the falling snow
>
> More faint that smothered voice of woe,
>
> *Excelsior !*

This was clearly abrupt in transition and
false also to the thought of the poem, for it
was no part of the poet's intention to char-
acterize the cry as a smothered voice of woe ;
so he rewrote it as it now stands, except that
in the second draft he wrote *startled air* for
frosty and *clear, cold* successively, a change
which added a new and striking effect. The

immense improvement in the new stanza is apparent at a glance, since in the turn of the poem the very action of the monks is subtly connected with the aspiration of the youth.

The first two lines of the last stanza but one gave the poet some trouble before he could find the most fit expression. In the first draft he wrote without erasure: —

> And guided by the faithful hound,
>
> A frozen, lifeless corse they found;
>
> Still grasping in his hand of ice
>
> The banner with the strange device,
>
> *Excelsior !*

In the second draft the first two lines appear:

> A traveller, by
> ~~Buried in snow~~ the faithful hound
> Half buried in the snow was
> ~~Far up the pass a traveller~~ found

The form in the first draft was probably chosen before the original seventh stanza was discarded. Certainly the omission of the pious monks in the final discovery is a gain; the loneliness of the youth is intensified when he is discovered not by one of his own race, but by a hound. Once more, as in the beginning, there is, as it were, a resolution into nature, and the youth, the snow and ice, and a dumb creature remain.

The first two lines of the last stanza stand in print as they were first written, but the last two lines show the poet's fatigue at the close of his work. He had his idea perfected, but his mind stumbled over the right words. Thus the first draft is as follows : —

> ~~And~~
> ~~His lips had caught the clear of day~~
>   serene
> And from the ~~deep~~ sky, ~~faint~~ and far
>   fell
> A voice ~~dropped~~ like a falling star,
>
>   *Excelsior!*

He did not know it then, but he had really finished his poem, for when he came later to write his second draft, he made his correction over again : —

>   serene
> And from the ~~deep~~ sky, ~~faint~~ and far

At the bottom of the first draft are the words, "September 28, 1841. Half - past three o'clock, morning. Now to bed." He wrote first September 27, and then remembered that he had reached the next day and changed the 7 to 8. If any one is curious to know the day of the week, it was Monday night that the poet sat up to write this poem. Sumner's letter to him is dated merely Thursday, so one can imagine that he had answered it and now had it lying by him as waste paper.

The study of the growth of a poem is an interesting and curious business, yet after all how little one really sees of the poet at work. Somehow or other, as Lowell says regarding Hawthorne, apropos of his note-books, you look through the key-hole and think you will catch the secret of the alchemist, but at the critical moment his back is turned toward you. It is rare, however, that one has so good an opportunity as this of seeing the shaping of a poetic idea.

EMERSON'S SELF.

FIFTY years and more have passed since the publication of *Nature*. Before the appearance of that little book, and for more than forty years after, Emerson's voice was heard in pulpit or on platform, with great frequency for a whole generation, and then intermittently, uttering those comments on things, men, and ideas which may be found under various arrangements in the eleven volumes of his collected writings. During this period, and with increasing attention, his thought has been made the subject of endless discussion, and has entered into the habit of other men's thought. It has stimulated, corrected, quickened, yet it has defied analysis, and it is vain to say that it has found, at the hands of any expositor, so clear a synthetic summary as to satisfy his readers.

In truth, there has been a general disposition to take Emerson as a large fact, and to require that he shall be treated in a large

way. A jaunty reviewer once proposed to
crush Wordsworth. "Crush Wordsworth!"
said Southey, with indignant scorn. "He
might as well try to crush Skiddaw!"   And
however one may cavil at Emerson, one cannot escape the conviction that the phenomenon of the New Englander is not to be
dismissed with an epigram. Time enough
has elapsed since he first came into view to
leave it quite certain that it is no longer a
question of degree of comparison with other
men, but of such tests as are applied to
unique men.

There is one mode of examination commonly used with writers which fails in the
case of Emerson. It has long been known
that the dates of publication of his works
offer slight criterion for dates of composition; indeed, that very few of his essays or
addresses have any such integrity as may be
implied in a preparation extending over so
much time as their length would require;
on the contrary, that they are all, or nearly
all, piecemeal productions, and a sentence in
one of late date may have been transferred
from a note - book of the earliest period.
Even with all the aid given by his biographer, it is impossible to make a chrono-

logical study of Emerson's writings with any
hope of reaching very definite conclusions
regarding the growth of his opinions. One
easily comes to think that there was little of
development, as we commonly understand
the phrase, — little, that is, of logical process by which a germinal thought comes to
maturity, and takes on a form very different
from its earliest expression ; but this does
not forbid that lateral expansion by which
certain large ideas, received with reference
to some one department of thought or action, spread so as to comprehend wide areas
of life. This is the gift of experience, and
the man of genius as well as the logician
may benefit by it.

Before the appearance of Mr. Cabot's
Memoir, the student was compelled to take
the body of Emerson's writings and treat it
as an impersonal subject, getting only such
oblique light as falls from a character more
than commonly dissociated from activity.
The Emerson whom all but his intimates
knew was a calm figure, living in the rustic
privacy of a New England village; appearing as a speaker to such audiences as would
gather to hear him ; occasionally mingling
on the platform with men and women of

some special organization, but himself identified with no sect or party ; touching many
movements in politics and religion, but not
at the centre of any of them ; separate, not
from want of sympathy, but through the
necessity of his nature. As the hands in the
fairy tale ministered to the wants of the
prince, though he saw no person, so the voice
of Emerson was always stealing out of the
mist which seemed to envelop him.

It is a matter for congratulation, that the
task of preparing the biography which was
to bring Emerson more distinctly into the
light, and reveal him even, I suspect, to
some who thought they already knew him
well, should have fallen to one who could be
intimate with Emerson's thought, and yet, in
his own mental habit, had a strong bent
toward systematizing. Mr. Cabot does not
assume the function of an interpreter who
conceives it his business to construct a con-
sistent Emerson, although he uses the topical method somewhat in treating of certain
marked phases of Emerson's thought and
life, such as transcendentalism and religion ;
but he shows himself to have that true historical method which marshals facts so that
they carry their own inevitable conclusions.

This is as valuable in biography as in history ; and while the manner of much contemporary biographic work is in the effacement of the biographer, the present subject is plainly one which calls for something more than a collection of letters and diaries. It demands a clear insight, a power to follow clues, and in general a capacity to bring a natural order out of what to many would have been a chaotic mass of material.

In this respect Mr. Cabot's *Memoir* is especially serviceable for supplying that one guide to a study of Emerson's works which was most needed : the disclosure, namely, of Emerson's conscious relation to his own thought. Mr. Cabot appears to have perceived the need, and to have lost no opportunity for adding to the image, which now stands in far clearer light than before, — the image of Emerson as he was to himself. Only as that is well apprehended may the student hope to solve some of the problems of Emerson's personality in its relation to the men and institutions of his time.

There is no break to be detected in the continuity of Emerson's life, scarcely any of those vacillations of purpose, those sudden

wayward impulses, which are like the change
of voice when a boy becomes a man. The
idealist was always there, and the genuineness of a style which was peculiarly his
becomes more apparent as one detects its
notes in his early letters. If he drew after
any pattern, it was that of his aunt, Mary
Moody Emerson, who seems to have entered
into his life more emphatically than any
one. Mr. Cabot points out one of the characteristics of her influence in forcing a certain concentration of intellectual life ; and
in speaking of it, he hints that all the Emerson boys suffered somewhat from the strain
laid upon them. " In Ralph's case the draw-
back came in another shape. Want of ' that
part of education which is conducted in the
nursery and the playground, in fights and
frolics, in business and politics,' — leaving
him without the help of the free-masonries
which these things establish, — no doubt exaggerated the idealist's tendency to fence
himself off from contact with men, and
made it an effort for him, in after-life, to
meet them on common terms in every-day
intercourse." Yet this was but a miniature
of his whole life. Once and again in his
writings, as instanced by the brief quotation

just given, Emerson looks wistfully toward
the solid ground on which he sees his fellow-
men walking, while he himself, by some
fatality of his nature, must needs move
above the surface. " The man of his aspirations," as Mr. Cabot well says, " was not
the moralist, sitting aloof on the heights of
philosophy, and overlooking the affairs of
men from a distance, but the man of the
world, in the true sense of the phrase ; the
man of both worlds, the public soul, with all
his doors open, with equal facility of recep-
tion and of communication." This, as I
said, is suggested by his writings, but it is
even more clearly brought out in his correspondence.

To his aunt Emerson wrote, always sure
of a recipient of his thought, and some
measure of her influence over him may be
taken by the freedom and fullness with
which he tried his speculations on her.
Hence, also, his letters to her are especially
valuable as marking the high tide of his
mind, and disclosing movements more important for making up an estimate of his nature
than he was probably aware. Thus there is
a fine letter to Miss Emerson, written when
he was loitering in Alexandria, on a return

from a health-seeking trip in the South. Emerson was twenty-four years old at the time, had just apparently found his place as a preacher, and was looked upon with growing interest in this capacity. " It occurs to me lately," he writes, " that we have a great many capacities which we lack time and occasion to improve. If I read the *Bride of Lammermoor*, a thousand imperfect suggestions arise in my mind, to which if I could give heed, I should be a novelist. When I chance to light upon a verse of genuine poetry, — it may be in a corner of a newspaper, — a forcible sympathy awakens a legion of little goblins in the recesses of the soul, and if I had leisure to attend to the fine, tiny rabble I should straightway be a poet. In my day-dreams I do often hunger and thirst to be a painter ; besides all the spasmodic attachments I indulge to each of the sciences and each province of letters. They all in turn play the coquette with my imagination, and it may be I shall die at the last a forlorn bachelor, jilted of them all. But all that makes these reveries noticeable is the indirect testimony they seem to bear to the most desirable attributes of human nature. If it has so many *conatus* (seekings after), as the philosophic term is, they are not in vain, but point to a duration ample enough for the entire satisfaction of them all."

Here the conclusion interests us less than the hint which the whole passage gives of Emerson's appropriation of the world, of his growing sense of power and his expansion of nature. It was not an argument for immortality which he was constructing; it was an attestation of his own indestructible personality. He was aware of the movement of his wings; he felt them beat the air; physically he was weak, but he was already testing his spiritual body, and discovering what reaches of vision and flight were possible to it. The very experience of a first journey from home, and especially of that return which always quickens the pulse of a live man, reinforced this interior excursion, and produced an exhilaration which may have been momentary in its extreme exaltation, but clearly marks an epoch in Emerson's spiritual life. Listen to the confidence which he commits to his diary at the same time: —

"*June*, 1827. Although I strive to keep my soul in a polite equilibrium, I belong to

the good sect of the Seekers, and conceive
that the dissolution of the body will have a
wonderful effect on the opinions of all creed-
mongers. How the flimsy sophistries that
have covered nations — unclean cobwebs
that have reached their long dangling threads
over whole ages, issuing from the dark bow-
els of Athanasius and Calvin — will shrink
to nothing at that sun-burst of truth! And
nobody will be more glad than Athanasius
and Calvin. In my frigidest moments,
when I put behind me the subtler evidences,
and set Christianity in the light of a piece
of human history, — much as Confucius or
Solyman might regard it, — I believe myself immortal. The beam of the balance
trembles, to be sure, but settles always on
the right side. For otherwise all things
look so silly. The sun is silly, and the connection of beings and worlds such mad non-
sense. I *say* this, I say that in pure reason
I believe my immortality, because I have
read and heard often that the doctrine hangs
wholly on Christianity. This, to be sure,
brings safety, but I think I get bare life
without."

The whole period bounded in his life by
his entrance upon the ministry and his resig-

nation of his charge is interesting for the
hints which it gives of the working of his
mind. Those eight years were the making
of Emerson. Then he seems to have found
his latitude and longitude, and his after-
life was in the main the expansion of the
thoughts then entertained. It is a pity
that his poems are not dated. They could
scarcely have been so desultory in composition as the essays ; and even if they were
subjected to revision and verbal changes, the
thought in each could hardly have been
altered. I am greatly mistaken if they
would not throw interesting light on the
recondite subject of Emerson's growth in
consciousness.

Emerson's desire to preach continued for
some time after it had been demonstrated
that there was no place for him in the institutional ministry. He seems to have made
several efforts to adjust himself to his fellows through this form of association, and at
last to have retired, baffled. In the condition of affairs in New England at the time,
the ministry seemed to be the only possible
profession for such a nature as Emerson's,
and in working into it and working out of it
Emerson may be said to have been following

an experimental course, hardly conscious of
its full significance. He was finding himself by the process of elimination, and it is
an interesting commentary on New England
life, as well as upon Emerson's personality,
that this long and somewhat costly experiment should have been deemed necessary.

The ministry was then, as it always had
been in New England, the one recourse for
the idealist. Literature there was none, and
there was no literary vocation. In the
intellectual growth of this province, so intense in its activity, and so comparatively
independent of growth elsewhere, there had
been a slow differentiation of functions
going on. Not long before Emerson's time
the minister had released the politician and
the lawyer, and these were now separate persons. In Emerson's time itself a further
separation took place, and the man of letters
stood distinct. Emerson was an agent in
this development, and as a consequence the
choice in many minds between the ministry
as a profession and the profession of letters
is made earlier in life, and without that long
experimental process which took place in
Emerson's case.

The very provincialism of the New Eng-

land mind, while it enlarged the scope of
the ministerial office, and caused that it
finally was capable of dividing itself into
several distinct offices of the higher life,
missed the one fundamental, ineradicable
notion of the ministry as disclosed in historic Christianity. It is interesting to note,
therefore, that the rock of stumbling, which
put an end to Emerson's ecclesiastical career,
was his inability to bring his congregation to
take the one little step, which seemed so
short, of giving up the sacrament of the
eucharist. Refined as that sacrament had
become in the conception of the people, it
still held them sufficiently to forbid their
treating it as unessential. To Emerson,
who was an individual, and very lightly
bound even by the association of his order,
the step was not only easy, it was necessary.
Individuals can always do what commu-
nities cannot, and Emerson, in breaking the
last bond which connected him with institutional Christianity, was following his destiny, as the society which could not break
this bond was half blindly obedient to a law
which each member of the society, if isolated by thought as Emerson was, might
have also disregarded. Emerson, in eman-

cipating himself from the ministry, was freed from a profession ; and since the ministry had come to be regarded simply as a profession, which one might choose as he chose the law or medicine, he was fulfilling the behest of that voice within him whose whispers we have already noticed. To him, as to most of his associates, the ministry was no longer regarded as an order. All the while that he was under the cloak of this profession he was more or less consciously struggling to escape, and one detects in his observations on preaching the rapidly increasing self-knowledge which was soon to make it impossible for him to remain in the pulpit. Thus he notes in his diary at the outset : —

" *Sunday, April* 24, 1824. I am beginning my professional studies. In a month I shall be legally a man ; and I deliberately dedicate my time, my talents, and my hopes to the church. . . . I cannot dissemble that my abilities are below my ambition ; and I find that I judged by a false criterion when I measured my powers by my ability to understand and criticise the intellectual character of another. I have, or had, a strong imagination, and consequently a keen relish for the beauties of poetry.

My reasoning faculty is proportionably weak; nor can I ever hope to write a Butler's Analogy, or an Essay of Hume. Nor is it strange that with this confession I should choose theology; for the highest species of reasoning upon divine subjects is rather the fruit of a sort of moral imagination than of the reasoning machines, such as Locke, and Clarke, and David Hume."

Here is a fumbling about, with his hand near, but not on, the handle of his being. Mark, now, how three years later, in a letter to his aunt, he has got upon the track of himself: " I preach half of every Sunday. When I attended church on the other half of a Sunday, and the image in the pulpit was all of clay, and not of tunable metal, I said to myself that if men would avoid that general language and general manner in which they strive to hide all that is peculiar, and would say only what was uppermost in their own minds, after their own individual manner, every man would be interesting. Every man is a new creation, can do something best, has some intellectual modes and forms, or a character the general result of all, such as no other agent in the universe has: if he would exhibit that, it must needs be engaging, must be a curious study to every inquisitive mind. But whatever properties a man of narrow intellect feels to be peculiar he studiously hides; he is ashamed or afraid of himself, and all his communications to men are unskillful plagiarisms from the common stock of thought and knowledge, and he is of course flat and tiresome."

Finally, an entry in his journal at the beginning of the year in which he resigned his charge marks the last stage in his evolution as he is about to emerge from the chrysalis of the New England ministry: "*January* 10, 1832. It is the best part of the man, I sometimes think, that revolts most against his being a minister. His good revolts from official goodness. If he never spoke or acted but with the full consent of his understanding, if the whole man acted always, how powerful would be every act and every word! Well, then, or ill, then, how much power he sacrifices by conforming himself to say or do in other folks' time, instead of in his own! The difficulty is that we do not make a world of our own, but fall into institutions already made, and have to accommodate ourselves to them to be useful at all; and this accommodation is, I say, a loss of so much integrity, and of course of so much power. But how shall the droning world get on if all its *beaux esprits* recalcitrate upon its approved forms and accepted institutions, and quit them all in order to be single-minded? The double-refiners would produce at the other end the double-damned."

This last sentence is a felicitous expression of an eddy in his mental current, but he goes straight at the practical question which his whole nature was asking when, a few days later, he writes with great force and with profound intelligence of his own spiritual quandary: "Every man hath his use, no doubt, and every one makes ever the effort, according to the energy of his own character, to suit his external condition to his inward constitution. If his external condition does not admit of such accomodation, he breaks the form of his life, and enters a new one which does. If it will admit of such accommodation, he gradually bends it to his mind. Thus Finney can preach, and so his prayers are short. Parkman can pray, and so his prayers are long. Lowell can visit, and so his church service is less. But what shall poor I do, who can neither visit, nor pray, nor preach, to my mind?"

Emerson broke the form of his life, and had to make a new one out of such stuff as his opportunities afforded. He lectured and he wrote, but in truth it mattered little just what form his occupation took. He had not left one profession to enter another; he had cleared himself of professional life altogether, and, having been true to the higher law of his being, he had that reasonable content thereafter which comes to one who has attained full power of consciousness. Emerson never came nearer to telling the whole truth about himself than when he wrote to his betrothed on the eve of their marriage, when discussing the comparative merits of Concord and Plymouth as places of residence: " I am born a poet, — of a low class without doubt, yet a poet. That is my nature and vocation. My singing, be sure, is very husky, and is for the most part in prose. Still I am a poet in the sense of a perceiver and dear lover of the harmonies that are in the soul and in matter, and specially of the correspondence between these and those. A sunset, a forest, a snow - storm, a certain river-view, are more to me than many friends, and do ordinarily divide my day with my books. Wherever I go, therefore, I guard and study my rambling propensities." And again, in speaking of the efforts of Greeley and Brisbane to attach him to their Fourierite association : "One must submit, yet I foresaw, in the moment when I encountered these two new friends here, that I cannot content them. They are bent on popular actions. I am, in all my theory, ethics, and politics, a poet, and of no more use in their New York than a rainbow or a firefly. Meantime, they fastened me in their thoughts to transcendentalism, whereof you know I am wholly guiltless, and which is spoken of as a known and fixed element, like salt or meal. So that I have to begin by endless disclaimers and explanations : ' I am not the man you take me for.' "

It is delightful to find in the *Memoir*, after the determination of vocation, repeated illustrations of Emerson's knowledge of himself, — that clear consciousness which he attained, not without effort, as we have seen, but also not with the violent throes of a man hardly born. The circumstances under which he came forward constituted the shell which he had to break, as I have tried to show, but his genius was always immanent, and prophetic from the start. Rarely, I think, has biography made so signal an addition to our power of knowing a man who had already made himself familiar through words. By Mr. Cabot's aid, it is as if a person with whom we had been talking for hours, who had endeared himself to us by the beauty and richness of his words and the nameless grace of his presence, should then unfold to us the process of his own spiritual being; not that which made him common with men, but that which gave him distinction, individuality. A revelation is afforded of the man himself in his self-discovery, in his expansion of nature, his growth of consciousness, in the very heart and secret of his genius.

An interesting comparison might be drawn, after the manner of Plutarch, between Emerson and John Adams. As Adams was the incarnation of the political New England, so Emerson was the finest product of that free-thinking New England which found no object outside the range of its speculation. The two were critical men. Adams came to the front in the crisis of political independence; Emerson in the crisis of religious independence. Theodore Parker was the wind which stormed against the conventionally religious man, and only made him draw his cloak closer about him; while Emerson, shining and smiling, made him loosen his robes and bare himself to the open air. With what a striking contrast of mood the two historic Americans passed out of ken! Adams, stormy even in his reminiscence of life from the quiet harbor of old age; Emerson, unperturbed when receiving the angry criticism of his day, subsiding into a long reverie of peace!

The visit of Emerson to England was the return of New England to the mother country in a more emphatic sort than was Hawthorne's. Never does England seem farther away from America than when one is reading *English Traits*. Below the surface of shrewd observation one may catch sight of the Spirit of England driven across the Atlantic two hundred years before, given new environment, set upon the same questions and bidden ask them in the open air, and getting its answer in such wise as to make everything strange when revisiting its old haunts. The individuality of Emerson, testing and trying England, is sharp enough, if one looks only for that, but it is easy also to resolve it into a speakership for a new people.

It is, however, in the attitude of Emerson toward his own countrymen that his personality is most interesting.   With all his written and spoken words concerning America, — and it is impossible to read his *May Day* without perceiving how great a relief to him was the return of peace after the separating war, — one fails to find the evidence of any passionate devotion to his country.   The service which John Adams rendered in his loyalty to the nation, which he saw less by imagination than by an heroic, steady realization of the facts of human life about him, was such a service as racked the giver. Emerson, in speaking of the volume of *Letters and Social Aims* which Schmidt introduced to the German public, used the expression "village thoughts."   A piece of slightly conscious humility must not be taken too gravely, yet the estimate really does partially set off Emerson's defect on this side. He was at home in Concord.   Anywhere else he was a stranger.   Even Boston was a place to visit, though he gave that city an affection which is embodied in some noble verses.   The glimpses which we get of the poet on his travels in his own country serve to deepen the impression which we form of

the purely spectacular shape of the country
in his vision. He was not indifferent to the
struggles going on, and yet they were rather
disturbances to his spirit than signs of a
life which quickened his own pulse.

To some minds this may seem to lift Emerson above other men. In my judgment
it separates him from them to his own loss.
It is precisely this passion of nationality
which differentiates seers and poets. Mil-
ton had it. Carlyle had it. Tennyson has
it. Victor Hugo had it. Goethe did not
have it. The absence of this passion is indeed the sign of an inferior ethical apprehension. At any rate, the passion for country is never far removed from the passion of
righteousness. The cry over Jerusalem was
the last echo of those prophetic voices which
make Israel and Israel's God to be joined
by closer than human ties. When one col-
lects his God from ethnic fragments he is
very apt at the same time to distribute his
country.

When all is said, there remains that
about Emerson which cannot be defined or
analyzed, — that bouquet of personality
which lingers in one's recollection of him,
whether one has acquired a knowledge of him

by personal contact or through his books and letters. Dr. Holmes says finely that there was " a sweet seriousness in Emerson's voice that was infinitely soothing." "I remember," he adds, " that in the dreadful war-time, on one of the days of anguish and terror, I fell in with Governor Andrew, on his way to a lecture of Emerson's, where he was going, he said, to relieve the strain upon his mind. An hour passed in listening to that flow of thought, calm and clear as the diamond drops that distill from a mountain rock, was a true nepenthe for a careworn soul." This is the impression which Emerson's nature leaves most ineradicably on the mind. The serenity of his life and thought was a great gift to his countrymen. The figure which they call up to mind always has a smile playing about the eager features; the voice that they hear is modulated and penetrating.

ASPECTS OF HISTORICAL WORK.

Von Ranke, after turning ninety, keeps cheerfully on with his Universal History; a score or more of learned men associate themselves in writing the history of a single American town. Which is the truer method? Which produces the better results? The answer depends greatly on what one wants of history. If it be a broad view of the stream of tendency, then a philosophical historian like Von Ranke, who has the insight, the power of seeing the end from the beginning, the perception of ruling ideas, is the writer to surrender one's self to. But there are other attractions in historic study. There is the possibility of wresting from some limited series of events the secret of their cause and effect; the ever-elusive search after indubitable fact; the exercise of one's imagination upon the material thrown up by the spade of the independent investigator; the tracing of the foundation upon which some political community has built so broadly as quite to hide from ordinary sight the source of its power. If one cares for history in this fashion, then nothing will content him save to get as closely as possible at the original documents and monuments of history.

There is another aspect in which history presents itself somewhat different from either of the above. It is an interesting story, not fabricated in the brain of some clever inventor, but worked out by some invisible power through the activity of real men and women; it is a drama of persons, set upon the stage of the world, to be resolved into order by the selective power of the imagination; it is a succession of events, having now and then a denouement, only to go on once more in a new series. In the hands of a writer who has a clear sense of perspective, the history of a nation or of an epoch may become luminous, and as attractive as the story, the drama, or the narrative, which deals with imaginary beings.

Of the three methods of historical writing which answer to these demands of the student and writer,—the philosophical, the scientific, and the literary, — there can be little doubt that the scientific method is now at the front. It agrees most perfectly with the spirit which dominates all departments of intellectual activity. George Eliot in her *Middlemarch* turned restlessly from one to another of her characters, in the hope of finding one that was built upon an unyielding foundation. Caleb Garth was the only one whom she heartily admired and respected. He was wont to speak of business, as many of religion, with reverence and a profound sense of its reality and comprehensive power. His character is built from this idea and for the expression of it. He is the incarnation of that consciousness of reality in one's self and firm fulfillment of the end of one's being which is the *cry* of *Middlemarch*. The historian is impelled by the same spirit which drove George Eliot. He wishes to get down to hard pan. He is skeptical, not as one who doubts from choice, but from necessity must push his inquiries until he comes upon the last analysis. Hence the historical student of the day is after facts, and he is ready to put his hook into any unlikely dust heap, on the chance of laying bare a precious bit. There is patience in the sifting of historical evidence, steadfastness in the following of clues, and a high estimate of the value of accurate statement.

I have instanced George Eliot as an example of the scientific spirit, because the historical student joins with the creative novelist on one side, with the scientist on the other. It is impossible to exclude human nature from history, and the historian dealing with the concrete facts of human activity is sure, sooner or later, to part company with the physicist or biologist who is engaged upon the dissection and classification of facts belonging to inorganic matter, or to organic matter below the order of man. The archæologist, groping about in the cave after the guttural-voiced dweller with his club and his little stone chips, trying to make out how the poor devil lived, and what he thought of the world into the light of which he had scarcely crept, may use the same method as his brother-worker who is measuring the wings of a paleozoic cockroach, but he is in a vastly wider range of human sympathy, and may give points to a Shakespeare reflecting upon Caliban and Setebos.

The most important illustrations of the scientific method as applied to American history are undoubtedly the two coöperative

works edited by Mr. Winsor. The general
scheme of the two works is the same.
That is to say it is conceded that no
one writer is able to compass a great
historical subject on all sides, but that the
work of a number of writers, each viewing
the subject from his own angle, may be so
arranged and made interdependent as to
form a conspectus of the whole. In the case
of Boston, Mr. Winsor had an admirable
opportunity for applying the coöperative
method of historical writing. He could sur-
round himself at once by a strong body of
special students. More research had been expended upon the history of Boston than upon
the history of any other town in the country. A well-organized and active historical
society could be drawn upon for aid and
advice ; there was an honest local pride to
be trusted for substantial encouragement.
More than this, the subject was one which
easily permits of disintegration. There is, it
is true, even about an American city a
certain organic life which is capable of
development in historic writing, and Boston
was for a long time a very individual and
conscious organism. Nevertheless, it is easy
to see what limitations there are to such a

view of any modern town, and how possible it is to resolve the forces of even so vital an entity as Boston into their constituent parts. Hence there was no insuperable difficulty in getting a sectional study of the town, especially as by the plan adopted the treatment of a topic was carried forward, volume by volume, through the successive periods of colonial, provincial, and state life.

The eminent success of the experiment upon the history of Boston justified the confidence of the editor in adapting his scheme to a continental subject. The *Narrative and Critical History of America* is a series of monographs treating of the western continent. This is a long step from the history of one town in America, and yet a moment's consideration will show that by making his coöperative history one of America instead of one of the United States, Mr. Winsor has simply enlarged the field of his historic method; he has not applied that method to a different kind of subject, as he would have done if he had undertaken to prepare the history of the United States in this way. For America is even less of an organism than Boston. Whatever the far-off ages may show of one increasing purpose, it is out of the question for an historian to marshal the moving forces of the western continent into any orderly sequence, with any controlling aim. The goal is altogether too far away for any historic survey to use it as a measuring point.

I do not believe it would be possible to write a history of the United States upon such a plan as Mr. Winsor has adopted in these two great works, because a topical treatment would inevitably fail to convey a notion of that organic development of national life which is the last and finest disclosure of historical composition. But a cyclopædic work on America, which follows the broad lines of chronology, is not only possible, but by such a treatment alone can justice be done to the subject. History, as told in this manner, will have a new charm for many minds, for the scientific mind is found in the public that reads, as well as in the students who explore.

But such monumental works as these inevitably suggest questions to the historical student. The thoroughness with which the ground is covered, the patience with which the cartography has been developed, the careful array of authorities, all these elements give the works a solidity and impressiveness which both stimulate the student and discourage him. The foundation laid for historical study in an independent manner is admirable, but a cursory examination may well lead one to despair of attacking history as a study, unless he is to confine himself to an exceedingly minute field. This, I say, is the first impression likely to be made upon the expectant student, and if it warns off all merely desultory speculators and indolent minds much is gained. But for the conscientious explorer and critic the stimulus afforded by any stout piece of historical work is very great, and in the face of such enterprises I am tempted to ask what fields lie open to the writer whose taste leads him to specialized work, and whose preference is for American subjects.

A main use to which such a coöperative work as the *Narrative and Critical History of America* will be put suggests one answer. It will serve as the index to historical material from which the popular writer will construct the story of history. It is not from such a work that popular ideas of our history are directly formed, but from the school-books, the magazine articles, and general histories. The sleepless vigilance of the custodians of historical material is the price paid for accuracy of general knowledge; and the work of the scientific student, so much of which is out of sight, consists largely in that critical examination of documents and monuments, the results of which, when clearly published, become the property of generalizing, philosophical, and literary historians. There is a work to be done, therefore, by the American scientific historical student, of real importance in the preparation of thoroughly edited series of papers relating to American history. The papers in the cabinets of historical societies, the letters which have accumulated in families, the records of towns and states,—there is a vast abundance of this material which ought to be patiently sifted and wisely set forth. One is in despair before a huddle of historical material, but he has a fine enthusiasm for work when he sees that same material ordered, classified, and indexed.

I look confidently for a class of critical scholars who shall expend unreserved labor upon authoritative editions of the writings of the men who translated the logic of events into the logic of words. It cannot be said that the fathers of the republic have been neglected. Washington, Franklin, Adams, Jefferson, Madison, Monroe, Hamilton, Sam. Adams, John Quincy Adams, have all been preserved in stately octavos; but the work done upon their writings was for the most part done rather to preserve manuscripts than to give scholarly presentation. Moreover, since the publication of these works, much new material has come to light both for completing the original documents and for purposes of illustration.

Take the case of Franklin for example. We cannot be said ever to have neglected Franklin. Editions of his writings and independent lives mark the interest of Americans in this wonderful exponent of his generation, an interest which was remarkable during his lifetime, has never diminished, and is now rising on a fresh wave. But where is the really satisfying edition of his writings? It may be that the time has not come for it, but I please myself with thinking that the work will be done finally under some such conditions as governed in the case of Francis Bacon's works. In justice to Franklin two editors are required, one of whom shall be qualified to treat him as a physicist, the other as a philosopher, statesman, and literary artist. Mr. Spedding's treatment of *Bacon's Occasional Writings* affords a capital illustration of how Franklin might be edited. It will be remembered that though the original literary partnership was Spedding, Ellis, and Heath, Mr. Spedding remained as the sole representative of the firm when the final division of Bacon's writings was published. His method was to print the letters, speeches, and miscellaneous writings in chronological order, connecting them with threads of narrative and explanatory comment. The writings afforded a fairly good survey of Bacon's personal life, but when thus connected and annotated, they furnished a splendid *Life and Times of Francis Bacon.* This is what ought to be done for Franklin. The fact that he wrote no one great work, — great, that is, in volume,— that his life from beginning to end is marked by tracts, letters, parables, essays, and philosophical discussions, and that he was a central figure on two continents, makes it possible to follow Mr. Spedding's admirable method to perfection. The occasional papers of Bacon after all gave only a partial view of the man ; the writings of Franklin, without classification, but taken chronologically, would give under this treatment the most thorough-going, continuous view possible of a great man and a great historic movement.

By the labors of scientific students the foundations are laid upon which other men build. Von Ranke, with his colossal industry, is a signal instance of a man at once minute in his detailed work and philosophical in his broad generalization ; but the combination rarely is found, and the philosophical historian shows his indebtedness to the individual sappers and miners. It is a fortunate thing if he admits this indebtedness in his own mind, and is willing patiently to use the labors of others. The temptation of the philosopher is to follow some enticing theory, especially if it promises to lead him away from generally accepted historical truths. Niebuhr says in one of his lectures that he is very suspicious of paradoxes, that it is the κοινὴ δόξη, the common opinion which is to be relied upon in historical matters, meaning that the consensus of historians is to be respected beyond any striking view which has novelty for its chief merit.

Yet there is such a thing as a slow revolution even in common opinion, the formation of a new habit of thought. Thus it was once the custom among American writers to treat American history as if it were exceptional, the product of forces integral to American life, and independent of European development. A sort of intellectual high tariff shut out foreign ideas, and encouraged the production of native notions. Such an attitude has given way before the impulse which is sending our students to the search for the beginning of institutions, laws, and organisms. A wiser understanding sees that for a considerable period, indeed down to the close of the second war with England, American history was in reality a part of European history, and could be truthfully related only by a person who took his stand now on one side, now on the other of the Atlantic. A truly philosophical history indicates those undercurrents of race, law, and institutions which make the nexus of the new world with the old, and act as interpreters of the later history, wrought out under more separate influences.

Nor is this all. If the writer of American history needs to throw open his windows toward the east, it is quite as needful that he should regard the aspect of our development which looks away from Europe. A delicate illustration of this is offered in the work of that new school of historical writers which puts The People in the titles of its books. The late Mr. J. R. Green was not precisely a pioneer, but his brilliant history was so conspicuous an example of a mode of treatment which commends itself to the minds of men educated under democratic principles, that it has served to stimulate other writers and to make historical students take much more careful note than formerly of the multitudinous life which finds expression in the varied form of human activity, and to cease concerning themselves mainly with governmental development. The rise of this school is a distinct witness to the new reading of humanity which the present century has known. The growth of democratic ideas has given dignity to the study of the individual; the emancipation of the intellect, which is a part of the great renaissance of modern times, has resulted in an intense inquiry into the reign of law: so that the most acceptable historian of to-day, the one most in accord with the temper of the age, is he who is able to detect the operation of the greatest variety of individual life, and to discover the comprehensive laws which govern in the development of the nation.

A country like England, where the idea of government by class has not so much been overthrown by the violence of revolutions as displaced by the greater energy of democratic principles, offers a most attractive theme to the historian who would disclose the undercurrent of popular life and its gradual emergence into the light of day. A history of the English people is a protest against an interpretation of history which makes it the drama of kings, and its finest success is in tracing a confessed power back into periods when it was dumbly, unconsciously, working out its destiny. Dean Stanley, leading a party of working men through Westminster Abbey, and discoursing upon the historical monuments to which they are heirs in common, is a fine picture of modern England; but by what steps were the figures in the picture brought together? To tell that is to tell the history of the people of England.

The contrasts which such a picture suggests are abundant in English history, and they arrest the mind; but is there an equally

suggestive theme in American history? Is
the history of the American people a protest
against false views of that history, which
once prevailed? Certainly not in so distinct a degree as may be averred of English
history, although the habits of historical
writing prevalent in one country have naturally influenced and largely determined the
same habits in the other. A recent American writer, for example, strikes a note in
the prelude to his history which betrays the
influence under which he has worked. " In
the course of this narrative," he says at the
outset, " much, indeed, must be written of
wars, conspiracies, and rebellions; of presidents, of congresses, of embassies, of treaties,
of the ambition of political leaders in the
senate-house, and of the rise of great parties
in the nation. Yet the history of the people
shall be the chief theme." I do not believe
that any American historian can go deeply
into such a subject without revising his
judgment as to the comparative unimpor-
tance in history of wars, conspiracies, rebellions, presidents, congresses, embassies, treaties, ambitions of political leaders, and the
rise of great parties. The ease with which
this writer sets all these aside is a mere

rhetorical burst, borrowed from the creed
of the school to which he belongs.   It is
very true that in English history there is a
people in distinction from a government,
but no one can make an exhaustive study of
United States history without revealing the
fundamental doctrine that the people con-
stitutes the nation, and that there is no political order external to it.   No doubt this
truth is one which grows clearer in the progress of the nation, and yet the organic life of
the people of the United States has always
been an integrity ; it is merely a habit of
mind borrowed from traditional study, which
speaks of wars, presidents, congresses, and
the like as if they were something foreign
from the life of the people, or only inci-
dental to it.   There is a radical defect in
any conception of the history of the United
States which invests the political life and institutions and administration of government
with any foreign property.   It is a defect
resident in much of our political thought,
and it is slowly wearing away from our
political consciousness ; its last stronghold is
in the minds of place-holders, but it ought
to be wholly absent from the mind of an
historical teacher.

There is, indeed, one view in which an
author governed by such a notion is in dan-
ger of missing the greatness of his subject
altogether. The history of a nation is
scarcely worth telling if it leave upon the
mind the impression that an improved mower,
or even a public school system, represents
its highest attainment. There is a national
life which surpasses any individual product,
or any system which human ingenuity has
evolved. It is in the realization of freedom,
and has its record in public acts and the deliberate registration of the public conscience.
A bill of rights is a more admirable representation of the life of the people than letters
patent, and the organic unity of the nation
has been found to mean more to the individual member of the nation than any well-
ordered or comfortable life, however adorned
by the arts and graces of civilization. It is
for this reason that congresses and courts,
proceeding from the people and responsible
to them, may occupy the thought of an historian of the American people, with more
just propriety than the same subjects may
engage the attention of an historian of the
English people.

Then, if one really desires to take up the

subject of United States history in a philosophical spirit, what large opportunities
there are for absolutely new lines of work.
Who, for instance, has fairly disclosed the
meaning of racial currents? Who has made
clear the great migration, unsystematic, un-
organized, yet moving with resistless force to
take possession of western areas? Even that
old, apparently threadbare theme of the relation of the separate states to the union has
been discussed chiefly in its political and
legal bearings. Who has yet fully grasped
the subtler relations which find expression
in the changing moods of political consciousness?

There is a means of study which has fallen
somewhat into disuse that may well be com-
mended to those who are ambitious of writing American history. Nowadays, a vigorous training at college and university, with
a few terms under some German historical
master, finds favor as a proper preparation
for worthy historical work. But this intellectual course misses one important effect:
it does not necessarily depolarize the mind
and set it free from those intangible, tradi-
tionary beliefs and prejudices which color
the perception of life. How nearly impossi-

ble it is, for instance, for a New Englander
to divest himself of that circumambient atmosphere through which his ancestors have
been in the habit of regarding the development of our political life, and which seems
to him nothing else than the clear light of
heaven! Association with southern or western bred men at the university will do something toward enlarging his horizon, but after
all it is not reflected light, but change in the
point of view which is most needed.

Valentine in discourse with Proteus, who
apparently has been urging his friend to
stay at home, declares, —

"Home-keeping youth have ever homely wits;"

and Proteus's uncle in like manner advises
his nephew to set out on his travels. He
urges Panthino to importune Antonio

"To let him spend his time no more at home,
    Which would be great impeachment to his age,
    In having known no travel in his youth."

This, no doubt, was the temper which
Shakespeare found amongst English gentle-
men in the restless, enterprising age upon
which he had fallen, and Bacon in his essay
Of Travel supposes throughout the custom
of travel for educational ends. The English
gentleman of Elizabeth's time expected to

take part in the government of his country, and he traveled abroad because government meant emphatically dealing with the neighbors of the nation. The American historical student likewise has very decidedly to do with the government of his country, because it is his special function to illuminate the history which must be constantly intelligent to the people in order that they may govern wisely. For him there is an immense aid in the habit of what may be called historical and political traveling in distinction from geographical. His closet study would be immensely vivified and enlightened by slow and leisurely journeying through the country. Let any one write a general history of the United States, and he will find, if he be a Bostonian, that he will write of events which took place in Boston and its neighborhood with an animation and precision painfully in contrast with the vagueness which occupies his mind when he comes to write of the battle of New Orleans or the attack on Fort Sumter. In the one case, the whole background is in his mind's eye; in the other, he has only the diagram of a map or chart to help him. Beyond and above this, the historian who has been naturalized in different

sections of the union will have been naturalized in thought also.   Bacon would have his
young English gentleman "sequester himself
from the Company of his Countrymen, and
diet in such Places where there is good Company of the Nation where he travelleth."
The advice is commendable to the historical
student, who is by no means free from the
perils of insularity in thought.

One is tempted to think that the improve-
ments in modern thought mean a fresh start
in all fields of literary production.   It is easy
to delude one's self with the notion that science and scientific methods are working such
a revolution in intellectual life that the human race will one of these days accept a new
grand division of time, and antiquity will
reach down to the nineteenth century.   At
any rate, such is the logical deduction from
the sentiments of a good many *laudatores
temporis præsentis.*   But there is one thing
that survives all the changes that come over
men's modes of thought, and that is art.
How great the apparent difference between
the Parthenon and Chartres Cathedral, yet
how capable the human spirit is of appre-
hending the beauty of each!   It is so with
literary art, and one finds no inconsistency

in enjoying Homer and Shakespeare. There is in art an appeal which is undisturbed by the conflict of reason, or by great changes in mental processes ; and there is an art of history which leaves Herodotus secure when Rawlinson has said his last word, and keeps Clarendon alive though scientific historians have been busy over documents which he never saw. It is in vain to suppose that the new era of historic research and faithful collation of obscure authorities, the hunt for the beginning of things, the laying bare of foundations, is to put an end to that writing and reading of history which is akin to the writing and reading of poetry, the creation and enjoyment of all forms of art. Only this may fairly be asserted : that the historian who undertakes to recite the epic of a nation is put under heavier bonds to be faithful to minor details, and will be held more strictly accountable for any departure from accuracy. He will also be relieved of much waste of energy by the thoroughness with which the way is preparing before him. The indexes to history, which are increasing in number and efficiency, will make it possible for the literary historian to qualify himself for his task as he could not before, and will help to save him from those false generalizations which an insufficient familiarity with facts renders almost inevitable. And readers — there always will be readers who will surrender themselves to the charm which puts skepticism to sleep, and awakens the larger trust in the divine possibilities of human freedom.

ANNE GILCHRIST.

THERE is a personality in some people which is brought out most distinctly by relations held to others. Mrs. Anne Gilchrist was a woman of marked strength of character and self - reliance; yet her very individuality is most discoverable when one sees her, through the medium of her son's memorial, with her husband, with Blake, with her children, with Whitman, and with Mary Lamb. She is always herself, but then her self was a nature which obeyed the great paradoxical law of finding life through the loss of it. Mrs. Carlyle is quoted as saying, as she watched her neighbor breaking up her Chelsea home for a retirement in the country, that Mrs. Gilchrist would " skin and bury herself alive for the benefit of her children." Comparisons are apt to be unjust as well as odious, and the picture of Mrs. Gilchrist keeping the integrity of her life when most completely devoted to the life of others is striking enough without the aid of any contrasting picture, even if two neighboring households readily suggest such a contrast.

Anne Burrows was twenty-three years old when she married Alexander Gilchrist. Her father died when she was eleven, and she was left to the care of her mother. The family seems to have been one which held by the tenets of the evangelical school, and Anne's education was directed in accordance with these tenets; but the few glimpses which her son gives of her girlhood disclose the independence of mind which was afterward so marked an attribute. Apparently, her religious education was based upon a merely superficial presentation of traditional beliefs, and her vigorous intellect, refusing such nurture, took refuge in an extreme independence. It is no uncommon phenomenon when the dry individualism of Calvinism, detached from the deep personal experience which saves the creed, sends the dissatisfied pupil into a richer naturalism, but one which has missed the profound significance of a common Christianity.

In Alexander Gilchrist the thoughtful girl found a true companion, or, to speak more exactly, the husband found in his wife one who could give to his nervous, eager, literary activity the aid of a calm, sympathetic, and constant nature. Mrs. Gilchrist has sketched her husband's life in the second edition of the *Life of William Blake*, and brief as that sketch is it leaves upon the mind a tolerably sharp impression of the conscientious, thorough, and minutely curious character to which she was so happily joined. She gave him, we cannot help thinking, an element of repose, and he gave her both an intellectual stimulus, and, by the legacy of his unfinished work and their little children, an occupation and purpose which carried her through hard years and deepened the forces of her nature.

Mr. Gilchrist was an enthusiast in art, and a finely constituted hero-worshiper. He is principally known to readers by his *Life of William Blake*, the actual composition of which was practically complete before he was cut off by sudden death, although considerable editorial labor was afterward expended on the work by his widow and by the two Rossettis. Mrs. Gilchrist does not seem to have had any special training in artistic studies before her marriage, and her chosen literary tasks after she was done with

the Blake did not lead her into the field of
art. Her intellectual companionship with
her husband made her quickly intelligent
in such matters, and she followed his lead
with confident step; but we are impressed
rather by the large wisdom which saved
her from a mere sympathetic pursuit of
her husband's studies. While he was with
her, she thought with him and worked
with him. When he was gone, she finished
his task carefully, with sound judgment and
excellent taste. Then she devoted herself
to the next interest, and lived for years
to mould and guide her children's characters.

Her husband's hero - worship made him
naturally a biographer, and his fine perception, his quick sympathy, led him to choose
subjects upon which he could expend generous labor; he had, as Mrs. Gilchrist says,
a "strong sympathy with the unvictorious
fighters in the battle of life." With this
came easily a warm admiration for persons,
and a willingness to make himself of use to
them. The man who would hunt with unflagging zeal for everything which threw
light upon the career of the dead Blake was
no less ready to lend his time and fine pow-

ers of literary scent to the living Carlyle;
and thus it came about that a friendly acquaintance with the hero ripened rapidly
into an affectionate relation, and Gilchrist
proved a most helpful aid to the historian
in searching for portraits. The two families
became neighbors in Chelsea, and the son
prints interesting extracts from his father's
journal and correspondence, in which the
social and a little of the domestic life of
the Carlyles is pleasantly outlined in a
scrappy, disjointed fashion. It would not
be fair to judge Mr. Gilchrist by the random
notes which he made. They were plainly
intended as pegs for his own memory, and
some of the trivialities would doubtless have
either been omitted altogether, or replaced
by the fuller form which they would have
suggested to the writer, if he had used this
material itself.

Nevertheless, these pages relating to the
Carlyles help to bring out the personality
of Mrs. Gilchrist, and it is for this that
one is glad to have them. They show the
young couple in friendly and natural association with the older and more famous people
near them; and though Mrs. Gilchrist appears almost in the background, the reader

is constantly pleased with the glimpses he catches of her, — womanly, devoted, intellectually strong, yet never obtruding herself, and always preserving that calm, cheerful self-poise which must have made her, with all her privacy of life, the one person to whom the other three restless figures turned for a sense of repose and steadfastness. It was at this time, also, that the Rossettis were added to the circle of the Gilchrists' acquaintance, and both now and later there are pleasing expressions of Dante Rossetti's subdued intensity of nature.

It was through her husband and his literary occupation that Mrs. Gilchrist came into association with these and other notable persons, but her husband was rather the occasion than the cause of her friendships. When he was taken from her, and she buried herself in the country with her children, her former friends showed in many ways that they valued her for her own sake; and though she secluded herself, she kept on, as she had done before, quietly and with delicate discrimination, receiving into her life the best that presented itself. She does not seem to have read widely, but she was indifferent to ignoble literature. She did not make a crowd of friends, but, while open and receptive to all, she gravitated toward those best worth knowing and most worth holding. Thus to Brookbank came the Tennysons, and their coming is so pleasantly told by Mrs. Gilchrist in a letter that I give it here.

"I was sitting under the yew-tree yesterday, when Fanny came to me and put a card into my hand. And whose name do you think was on that card? If I were talking instead of writing, I should make you guess, and keep you in suspense a long while; but that is no use in a letter, because you can peep forward. It was 'Mr. Alfred Tennyson.' He looks older than I expected, because, of course, the portraits one was early familiar with have stood still in one's mind as the image to be associated with that great name. But he is, to my thinking, far nobler looking now, every inch a king: features are massive; eyes very grave and penetrating; hair long, still very dark, and, though getting thin, falls in such a way as to give a peculiar beauty to the mystic head. Mrs. Tennyson, a sweet, graceful woman, with singularly winning, gentle manners, but she looks painfully fragile and wan. . . .

"But what you will be most anxious to hear is all that he said. Mrs. Tennyson having mentioned that they had just come over from Petersfield, and that they had been there to see a clergyman who takes pupils, with an idea of placing their boys with him, when Giddy [a child of seven] came into the room, Tennyson called her to him, asked her her name, kissed her, stroked her sturdy legs, made Mrs. Tennyson feel them, and then set her on his knee, and talked to her all the while I was over at the Simmons' arranging matters. Afterwards, when we were walking up a hill together, he said, 'I admire that little girl of yours. It is n't every one that admires that kind of very solid development of flesh and blood, but I do. Old Tom Campbell used to say that children should be like bulbs, — plenty of substance in them for the flower to grow out of by and by.' Tennyson asked me how many children I had; and when I said 'four,' answered hastily, 'Quite enough! quite enough!' at which I was not a little amused."

So began a pleasant friendship, which was confirmed when the Tennysons came to stay in the neighborhood, and Mrs. Gilchrist made herself a most hospitable and helpful neighbor. Her letters at this time give most agreeable bits from Tennyson's talk, and unwittingly show how much the poet respected this cheerful, serene, and hard-working mother. Hard-working indeed she was. A strict economy was needful, and everything was to be done for the children. It was for them that she had sought this country seclusion, and she was giving them not only the physical training which the pure air and sweet country permitted, but the careful training in mental power which her strong nature made possible. All else was subordinate; and while she used her pen from time to time, to add to her slender income, she resolutely measured her strength with regard to the one crowning purpose of this part of her life. She writes to her sister-in-law : —

" Masson has accepted the article I wrote last spring [*The Indestructibility of Force,* in *Macmillan's Magazine*]. And that will be the last thing I shall attempt for many a long day, as I have fully made up my mind to give myself up wholly to educating the children. I find it such a harassing strain to attempt two things. Bad for me, because to be hard at work from the time you step out of bed in the morning till you step into it at night is not good for any one; it leaves no time, either, for general culture, for drinking at the refreshing fountain of standard literature and of music. Bad for the children, because it made me grudge them my time of an evening, when so much indirect good may be done to them by reading aloud and showing them prints. And after all they will not always be children; and if I have it in me to do anything worth doing with my pen, why, I can do it ten years hence, if I live, when I shall have completed my task so far as direct instruction of the children goes. I shall only be forty - six then, not in my dotage. Do you think I am right? A divided aim is not only most harassing to a conscientious disposition, but quite fatal to success — to doing one's very best in either." And later she writes of teaching "as real hard work, and I spend five hours a day at it; and then the amount of industry that goes to making two hundred a year do the work of four or five is not small. However, my prime rest, pleasure, society, all in one, — what keeps me going in a tolerably unflagging way, — are the glorious walks. Hind Head is as fresh to me as the day I first set eyes on it. And if I go out feeling ever so jaded, irritable, dispirited, when I find myself up there alone (for unless I have perfect stillness and quietness, and my thoughts are as free as a bird, the walk does not seem to do me a bit of good), care and fatigue are all shaken off, and life seems as grand and sweet and noble a thing as the scene my bodily eyes rest on; and if sad thoughts come, they have hope and sweetness so blended with them that I hardly know them to be sad, and I return to my little chicks quite bright and rested, and fully alive to the fact that they are the sweetest, loveliest chicks in the whole world; and Giddy says, 'Mamma has shut up her box of sighs.'"

The familiar intercourse which Mrs. Gilchrist maintained with the Rossettis, by interchange of visits and correspondence, gave occasion for an acquaintance which largely colors the latter half of the memorial of her life. Mr. William Rossetti introduced Walt Whitman to the English public by a volume of judicious selections, and one of its earliest readers was Mrs. Gilchrist, who wrote: "Since I have had it, I can read no other book; it holds me entirely spellbound, and I go through it again and again, with deepening delight and wonder." Mr. Rossetti at once placed the entire body of Whitman's verse in Mrs. Gilchrist's hands; and there followed a series of letters from her, which were a little later run into a consecutive article, printed in America, and reprinted in the memorial volume as *An Englishwoman's Estimate of Walt Whitman*. Mr. Rossetti introduced the letters by a brief note of his own, in which he characterized them as " about the fullest, farthest-reaching, and most eloquent appreciation of Whitman yet put into writing, whether or not I or other readers find cause for critical dissent at an item here and there. The most valuable, I say, because this is the expression of what a woman sees in Whitman's poems, — a woman who has read and thought much, and whom to know is to respect and esteem in every relation, whether of character, intellect, or culture." Fifteen years later Mrs. Gilchrist again summed her judgment of Whitman and his apostleship in a paper entitled *A Confession of Faith*.

There is, or rather was fifteen or twenty years ago, in England, a disposition among literary and artistic people of a distinct type

to construct an American phantom. The
men and women who were at odds with the
England of their day, impatient at smug
respectability, chafing not so much at the
petty restrictions of conventionality as at
the limitations imposed by institutional religion and politics, wishing to escape from
the commercial conception of the universe,
and met everywhere by the self-complacency
of Philistinism, took refuge in two widely
separate realities, mediæval romanticism and
American freedom. The one inspired their
art and much of their poetry, the other en-
kindled their thought. Both offered them
an opportunity to protest against English
lawful dullness. In America these spirits
saw the cheerful largeness of hope, the
confident step, the freedom from tradition,
the frank appropriation of the world as
belonging to Americans, and a general habit
of mind which proclaimed law as made for
man, and not man for law. With the ardor
of worshippers, the more *outré* their idol
the more they admired it. An exaggerated type of frontier lawlessness, some som-
brero-shadowed, cowhide-booted being, filled
them with special ecstasy. It was not that
they cared to go and live with him on the

prairie, but he served as a sort of symbol to
them of an expansive life which was gone
from England, but was possible to humanity. They knew he was exaggerated, that
there were cityfuls of people in America
who regarded him as a side-show; but he
brought the freshness of contrast with him,
and so served the end of their thought in
his way as effectively as a Cimabue did in
another. Cimabue and the latest wild man
of the West met in the London studio and
drawing - room, and though they did not
know each other had a " mutual friend."

Thus these dissatisfied Englishmen sought
in American literature for something new,
something that could not have been written
in London, and they were impatient of those
fine shades of difference which make American literature as distinct as Americans themselves, and just as defiant of analysis ; they
wished to see their conceptions of America
materialized in bold, unmistakable shape.
They did not ask for form, — they had abundance of that in England ; they asked for
spirit, and it might take any shape it chose.
So, persons whose artistic perception was
delicately developed accepted as a fact,
which transcended all ordinary laws of art,

poetry as huge, as floundering, as inorganic, as Blake's wandering visions, and like those visions shot through with superb lines, touched with gleams of heavenly beauty, suggesting waves of profound thought. Poetry broken loose was what they saw and admired.

There is much in the point of view, in admiration. From a London studio an American wonder will have a different aspect than from the interior life of America itself, and the explanation of the apparent indifference which his own age and country may show to a poet received with acclaim in a foreign land may be found in the very community which his contemporary countrymen enjoy with him. They see the thoughts which they think, and are all the while unconsciously translating into activity, rendered in a poetic form, which has little value for them precisely because it comes too close to their nature. They are accustomed to tall talk, and they treat it good-humoredly, as a weakness of their own. But because they are living freely, generously, and, if one may say so, splurgily, they instinctively seek form in their ideals of art, and demand that the spiritual forces which they admire shall have a completeness and precision complementary to their own somewhat vague and unrestrained life. It was no unmeaning accident, but a clear demonstration of this conscious want, which made sculpture the first effort of any consequence in American art. It was this perfection of form which endeared Longfellow to his countrymen, and it is the delicacy of art in Hawthorne which has made him so representative an American writer.

I have strayed a little from my immediate theme. Mr. Rossetti rightly congratulated himself that so strong a woman as Mrs. Gilchrist should welcome Whitman, and no one can read her own analysis of this new nature which had been presented to her without respecting her lofty courage and broad sympathy. " Perhaps Walt Whitman has forgotten, or, through some theory in his head, has overridden," she writes, " the truth that our instincts are beautiful facts of nature, as well as our bodies, and that we have a strong instinct of silence about some things." Having said that, she dismisses the matter, or rather proceeds to take up into a general philosophical *coup d'œil* all that in the poet which individually or in detail might offend her.

My business is not with the poet, but
with the woman, and my interest is in seeing how boldly she uses the poet as a whole
to carry forward her thought, to enlarge her
conceptions of human life, and to solidify
and define floating notions of science and
religion which had long been forming in her
mind. She was right, from her point of view,
in disregarding special criticism. It was
not whether Whitman, in this or that poem,
had given her pleasure or offended her sense
of propriety; he was to her, in the sweep of
his prose and verse, a democratic prophet,
and as such a most welcome guide into those
larger regions of thought whither her mind
was tending. She belonged to the larger
England of her day, and with a woman's
wit and fidelity she recognized at once and
accepted without reserve the Greatheart
who should point the way to the city of her
desire. Few phenomena in Mrs. Gilchrist's
life impress me as more indicative of her
womanliness than this strong passion for a
book which in its ordinary acceptation would
seem to repel rather than attract a woman's
nature. In a large way she was disclosing
the same noble nature which we have noted
under other conditions. She was losing her

life to find it; she was suppressing the individual in her to rise into the nobler conception of the humane life; and in giving herself so abundantly to a great idea — for it was a great idea which she caught through the medium of this new nature — she was enlarging and enriching her own personality. All this I can say, looking at the matter from her point of view, but I think she was wrong, fundamentally, in her philosophy; for naturalism, however far it may be developed, never has accounted, and never can account, for the sons of God.

I have dwelt so long on the more striking periods of Mrs. Gilchrist's development that I can only refer briefly to the circumstances that followed. In 1876 she came to America for two or three years, enlarging her circle of acquaintance, and as before quietly possessing herself of the best that came in her way; not restlessly seeking the unusual or the conspicuous, but looking with interest and a fine discrimination upon the life with which fortune brought her into contact. Naturally she sought out Walt Whitman, and established pleasant friendly relations with him. She found him fully realizing the ideal she had formed from his poems;

for Mrs. Gilchrist had a sane mind, and was abundantly able to take care of her conceptions.

The years which succeeded Mrs. Gilchrist's return to England, from 1879 to 1885, were filled with occupation. She wrote a sympathetic life of Mary Lamb for the series of *Eminent Women*, and some minor articles, and brought out a second and revised edition of the *Blake;* and she moved in a circle of friends who called out her cheerful help, and gave her in return the homage of respect and affection. She passed through a strong grief in the loss of a daughter, and her own strength, which had been undermined by years of devotion, gave way at last. In the somewhat fragmentary treatment of the memorial volume these last years are not very fully treated, but one is incurious of petty detail. He is satisfied with the sketch which is left on his mind of a woman notable not so much for any mark which she has left on the literature of the day, though, under other conditions, she might well have been eminent thus, as for the fine portrait which she presents of an English gentlewoman of the new yet ever old school, brave, honest, hospitable to the largest thought, devoted and genuine, with a serene cheerfulness under circumstances which strain the character. Nor is one, who knew her even slightly, ever likely to forget that fine presence, the dignity which could bear the added title of quaintness without offense, the equipoise of manner which told of an equanimity of life.

THE FUTURE OF SHAKESPEARE.

IT happens to the ingenuous traveller upon first visiting Switzerland to experience a shock to his sensibilities not many days after he has entered the enchanted region of mountains. As he climbs some gently ascending path, with the increasing exhilaration which the upper air engenders, he is suddenly confronted by a gate or some other bar to progress, and discovers that he must pay a franc, or half a franc, before he can make his way to the one point from which a wonderful view is to be obtained. He forgets at once the gentleness of the path by which he has climbed, in indignation at the mercenary spirit which has prompted the miserable owner of this particular part of the mountain to levy upon the lover of the picturesque. He fumes inwardly and possibly sputters outwardly as he pays the tax and passes on his way; the view to which he has become entitled, of which, indeed, he is now a sort of tenant, may be ever so grand, but it is vexatiously confused with the meanness of its peasant proprietor.

It is somewhat thus with our apprehension of Shakespeare. In imagination, more even than in reality, access to his meaning seems barred by the officiousness of commentators. The host of industrious scholars who have opened ways to desirable points of view are apt to seem to us rather impertinent toll-takers who will not let us into the delights and mysteries of our author unless we stop to read their notes and comments. I suspect that for a great many readers Shakespeare is an enchanted castle thickly beset by an impenetrable hedge of notes which has grown up especially during the past century so as to render the place quite inaccessible. Yet along comes the prince, riding gayly with the ardor of adventure ; the thorns and trees divide at his touch ; he passes the sleeping sentinels, enters the palace, discovers the princess, touches her lips, and without the blast of horn or bugle, the whole world of knights and ladies, servants, cooks, and scullions awakes to busy, joyous life. It was the princely nature only for which these drowsy folk waited, and the secret of Shakespeare yields to the gallant mind that goes straight to its mark.

Yet it would be a mistake to cheapen in our minds the work of the commentators. We should fare ill without them, and they are slowly but effectively constituting a new and important body of literature. Let any one read attentively the *Variorum* edition of *Othello* which Mr. Furness has so patiently and with such fine sense of proportion prepared for the use of the student. He will perceive what I mean when I venture to predict that the time will some day come for a new and interesting study of Shakespeare,— namely, the study of Shakespeare as reflected in successive generations of men. Acute minds will set themselves the problem of discovering not what Shakespeare was by himself, but what he was in the consciousness of other men,—the men of his own time, the men of Pope's time, the men of Coleridge's time, the men of Matthew Arnold's time. It will be a most curious and by no means unprofitable investigation, for it will add to the fullness and accuracy of our conception of mankind in a growth of its consciousness, the last and finest result of historical and philosophical study.

Already it is possible to indicate some of the broader marks of this reflection of

Shakespeare in the mirror of men's thoughts. It has been well said that in the days of the Restoration when Pepys found *Othello* a mean thing as compared with the intrigue-riddled play of *The Adventures of Five Hours*, Dryden was addressing the people of England through the ghost of Shake - speare. But Dryden found Shakespeare "untaught, unpractis'd, in a barbarous age;" with all his poetic admiration for the genius of this great progenitor, Dryden thought it meet and indeed necessary to veneer Shakespeare with a polish of his own.

A crasser critic in the time of Dryden, Mr. Thomas Rymer reflected better, it may be, the comonplaces of the judgment of the time when he says, speaking of *Othello*, "in the neighing of a horse, or in the growling of a mastiff, there is a meaning, there is a lively expression, and, may I say, more humanity, than many times in the tragical flights of Shakespeare."

What more distinctly indicates the absence of veneration for Shakespeare in this period than the fact that Dryden and Davenant altered the *Tempest* in order to introduce spectacular effects which should catch the eye and ear of a public that demanded sen-

suous delights? But this perversion of the
purest piece of imaginative fancy which the
world has ever seen held its place on the
stage for a hundred and fifty years. During that period there were other illustrations
of the persistent blindness with which people looked at Shakespeare. Colley Cibber
turned *King John* into *Papal Tyranny*, and
the drama mumbled denunciations of the
Pope and Guy Faux for a century with all the
toothless virulence of Bunyan's Giant Pope
himself. Tate remodeled *Lear* and over-
turned *Richard II.* into *The Sicilian Usur-
per*. The earlier editors of the text, which
began to be taken in hand near the beginning of the eighteenth century, were all busy
with trying to show what Shakespeare ought
to have said, not what he did say; and when
the critics of the text, as distinguished from
the critics of the stage, delivered themselves,
it was for a long time on the assumption
that Shakespeare was an uncouth, half barbarous writer, an outlaw utterly objection-
able to the rules of art, and the praise when
bestowed was very sure to be in the wrong
way and upon the wrong passages. Dr. Sam
Johnson dismisses *A Midsummer - Night's
Dream* with the words: " Wild and fan-

tastical as this play is, all the parts in their various moods are well written." We may sum the whole matter by remembering that Shylock, one of the most pathetic figures in the gallery of Shakespeare, was all this time received with shouts of laughter. The English public was as stupid in the main, up to the end of the last century, in its regard of Shakespeare as it has been to the present day in its apprehension of *Don Quixote* as a sort of crazy buffoon.

Nothing to my mind so distinctly marks the change in the consciousness of Englishmen which took place at the time of the French Revolution as the attitude toward Shakespeare and the Elizabethan dramatists in literature, and the new regard for mountains in nature. Gray was a forerunner of the new dispensation, and his perception of the imaginative element resident in mountain scenery, as opposed to the dislike of mountains for their rudeness which his companions entertained, was another form of the same spirit which took delight even in Icelandic and Gaelic poetry. The great consentaneous judgment, however, of Coleridge, Wordsworth, Lamb, Hazlitt, De Quincey, and lesser lights when dealing with Shake-

speare and Shakespeare's companions, marks
the real revolution in English thought and
sentiment. Wordsworth was not without
secret misgivings as to Shakespeare, and
Lamb was an open contemner of mountains,
but a common judgment, divided in its manifestations, impelled them to the same practical evangelization of the British mind. By
a natural course, there came first the juster,
truer insight into the nature of Shakespeare,
and then the desire to establish his text
upon critical, scientific principles. If the
labor of commentators during the past fifty
or sixty years has been more scrupu-
lously exact, it is because there was first
implanted a veneration for the poet. This
veneration has no doubt been often very
unreasoning, and there has been a disposition to make a fetich of Shakespeare, but
the great fact remains that in the present
consciousness of the English-speaking race,
Shakespeare is as firmly established, as sol-
idly set against any skeptical misgivings
of his greatness, as Mont Blanc itself. I
count this a very important position for
the human mind to have reached, since it
releases one from the necessity of elemen-
tary criticism, and gives the freest possible

scope for suggestive and what I may call constructive criticism. Grant that Shakespeare is great, and our business is to point out in what his greatness consists; our pleasure is to trace the form and content of his greatness.

But why dwell on this simple truth? Was there ever a time when Shakespeare was not considered great? No, there never was a time when single minds did not apprehend his greatness, but there was a long stretch of time when insolent use of him demonstrates a failure of men, in particular and in general, to recognize his commanding position in human art; and I repeat that the universal recognition of Shakespeare during the past two or three generations is both a symptom of advance in spiritual intelligence and also a prophecy of new movements of thought.

I think that textual criticism of Shakespeare has probably expended its force. Undoubtedly there always will be students whose habits of mind predispose them to this sort of work, and new and carefully edited texts will be published; but they will owe their importance chiefly to some peculiar advantage of mechanical arrangement, or typographical exactness ; and a new reading or emendation will be discussed and fought over out of all proportion to its value, simply because of the poverty of opportunity for such discussion. I think also that literary and historical illustration of Shakespeare, while affording a wider field and attracting fresher minds, has reached a point where the mass of material accumulated waits for careful sifting and ordering. Such a dictionary as Schmidt's indicates how this work of condensation and convenient presentation is going on, and new editions of Shakespeare are likely to owe their attractiveness to the skill with which the best of this material for illustration is employed.

What then remains for the Shakespeare scholar, eager to make his contribution toward the interpretation and fulfillment of this great body of literature which we know as Shakespeare's Plays ? And what is the direction which the Shakespeare study of the immediate future is likely to take ?

A partial reply could be made if we were to take into consideration a moment the change in attitude of the student of Shakespeare. While Shakespeare has remained the same for the past two centuries and a half, his reader has changed. Mont Blanc has been gladdened by sun and smitten by fierce storms, and enshrouded by clouds from the beginning, but it is only just beyond the memory of men, in modern times, that the mountain has been to the multitude anything but a phase of nature to recoil from. Yet now that Mont Blanc has become popular, in how many ways and by what various devices men express their interest in it. They climb its slippery sides, and suffer cold and hunger, and risk neck and limb, for one shivering hour on its summit; they peck at it with their geological hammers; they measure its crevasses; they analyze its snows; they photograph it; they climb the Montanvert to see it; they look at it from as many points of view as Mr. Pecksniff had for sketching Salisbury Cathedral; they write poems about it; and if they have not seen it at all, they imagine how it looks. There are as many Mont Blancs as there are educated Christians.

Now with all these individual apprehensions of the mountain, it is easy to see that there are certain groups of mind into which the apprehension may be classified; there is

the point of view of the tourist, of the geolo-
gist, of the artist, and all these points may ex-
ist in the minds of a single person. But after
we have set aside the special interest of the
scholar in Shakespeare and have accounted
for the taste of the philologist, the textual
critic and the student of dramatic and poetic
technique, there remains that large human
interest in Shakespeare which varies from
age to age as humanity itself changes its attitude toward whatever comes within its ken.
This change takes place in the mind of any
one person growing from childhood to maturity. As a child, one finds a story in Shakespeare, and the story may even be extracted
from the dramatic form as Charles and Mary
Lamb have done ; in the glow of youth, the
movement in Shakespeare, that great flow of
action toward an appointed end, is the current into which one throws one's self, and
happy is one so trained in freedom as to be
able to abandon himself to this swift, this
mighty tide. A little later comes the interest in persons, in the expression of character, in the evolution of thought, and along
with this a keen sense of the literary art,
the wit, the humor, the telling phrase, the
genetic word.

This is the stage last reached and always held by many, but there is a further interest in Shakespeare which comes to one here, another there, whose habit of thought is to find for all things transient some supernal, overarching, eternal counterpart of truth. What is philosophy but the never ending effort to make heaven and earth into one perfect sphere ?

" There are more things in heaven and earth than are dreamt of in your philosophy," says Hamlet, who has had the nether world suddenly opened to him, to the gallant, eager Horatio, the scholar and frank gentleman. Let Horatio also get a glimpse of these mysteries, and for him the old formulas of philosophy learned in the schools become half empty of meaning. It is, I say, the effort of earnest minds to translate into terms of lasting import the fleeting phenomena which assail them in their daily life in the world. Who of such has not felt the desire to get far enough away from the confusion of the present to secure a true perspective and see things as they really are, not as they appear ? Even distance in space sometimes affords almost the help of distance in time. If I were minded to write a history of modern America, a history of the past twenty years, I am sure I should find it of real service to take my stand bodily on the other side of the Atlantic. The questions which crowd upon us now in theology, in politics, in government, in science, make us crave some jutting crag of vantage from which to answer them.

To the mind seeking the solution of the great problems of human life, and asking for some definite expression of the problems themselves, there is always Shakespeare. In the microcosm which he offers one finds a miniature world just far enough away to permit a comprehensive study, just near enough to permit the warmth of humanity to be felt. The figures in the Greek drama are more sharply defined, and the action of human forces is more elemental; there are fewer complexities to distort the judgment. But this very simplicity, profound as it is, removes the world which it reflects to a distance from our sympathy and our practical thought. As an abstraction, the world of the Greek drama is held more firmly and yields to a finer logic, but we have to insist on the community of our humanity with it. It does not itself force this view upon us.

The world of Shakespeare, on the contrary, is not another planet in our system; it is our very world itself, reduced by literary art to a form which permits the most varied and the closest study of a great whole. It was Hawthorne, I think, who said of Trollope's stories that to read them was to get such a glimpse of current English life as one might get of the maggots in a cheese by cutting through its centre. The realism of Shakespeare is as powerful, as vital, as that of Trollope; but the moment we begin to compare the two, we discover the difference between a realism which merely reproduces the external world, and the realism which is the instrument of an art that contemplates wholes, and those wholes comprehensive of the spirit of man in its largest reaches.

It is the multiformity of Shakespeare's art, its complex illustration of human spiritual activity, that renders it so unfailing a resource to all who would read the mind of humanity, and who ask for some external and fit presentation of their thought. No doubt there are those who find Goethe's *Faust* a completer and more significant eidolon of their imaginative skepticism, and of *Weltschmerz*, but it is possible that the nineteenth century is accountable for this preference, and that *Faust*, for all it is so much of an air plant, will have a less vigorous clutch upon another century, while Shakespeare's plays, though rooted and grounded in the England of Elizabeth, will be read, not as antiquarian transcripts of an impermanent form of human life, but as enduring expressions of that which is most lasting in the human consciousness. Certainly, until the modern world is as far removed from Elizabeth by some cataclysm of moral forces as it now is from Pericles by the great fact of Christianity, Shakespeare will continue to reproduce for us ourselves and not another race of men.

Nevertheless, there is in Shakespeare, as in every great humanist, that which is local, transient, temporary, as discriminated from what is universal and eternal. We go to the commentators for explanation of allusions which have become obscure to persons living in Massachusetts to-day and not in Warwickshire when America was a far-away name. Beyond these linguistic and social changes, however, which scarcely interrupt the course of an intelligent reading, there are lapses in the great forms of human

society which cause us, if we are keen in
our sense of our own relations, to read the
plays which record Shakespeare's sense of
his human relations with a new interest, an
interest derived not solely from the vivid
appeal made to us by his characters and
their drama, but also from the light of
contrast thrown upon our own familiar experience. We do not, for example, find the
least difficulty in realizing the absurdity of
Malvolio's attitudinizing in cross-gartered
yellow stockings, although it is doubtful if
any base-ball team in the country ever
thought of adopting that sign-pedal, and
Slender's *Book of Riddles* does not need to
be translated for us into *Harper's Drawer*
before we can understand why the bashful
swain who had no wit of his own should
lean heavily on that which was provided for
him by the intelligible literature of the day.
But when the fun of *The Merry Wives of
Windsor* has expended itself, and we return
to our own social life, we find it somewhat
difficult to reproduce not the mere external
conditions of that drama, but the social
ethics to be translated into the terms of our
ordinary society.

What a capital opportunity, by the way,

this play offers for an ingenious study of
Shakespeare. I would suggest as a task
for any student in literature who wished
at once to study the great dramatist and
to perfect himself in the art which we all
secretly believe we can practice, — I mean
the art of writing a novel, — to take *The
Merry Wives of Windsor* and make of it
a novel under the title, say, of *Anne Page's
Lovers.* What he would need to do would
be to make Anne Page and her experi-
ences the central theme of the novel, throw-
ing Sir John Falstaff and the Merry Wives
into the background, treating their adventures and larks as the occasions out of which
Anne's opportunities spring. One who essayed this would be struck at once with the
change of interest which has come over the
world of men and women. To the audience
at the Bankside Theatre the centre of interest was Sir John and the roystering ladies
of the comedy. The figure of Anne Page
steals almost coyly across the stage. But
to-day the reader of the novel of *Anne
Page's Lovers* has his or her attention fixed
upon the girl and her budding life, — the
other figures skip about in the background
as amusing foils and illustrations of the
fatuous comedy of middle-aged sport.

The comparison of the drama and fiction is something more than a comparison of forms; it looks to an inquiry into the attitude of modern civilization towards human life; it tells us that there has sprung up a literature, immense in volume, which concerns itself with different subjects from those which engaged the attention of the masters of the drama; that it supposes a penetration of society in every direction; sinks its shafts through every stratum of social structure, in its eagerness to bring up ore from the lowest deposits. The extension of the novel into all the fields of human thought and action means a corresponding breadth of human inquiry; authors and readers together, sustaining this vast literary organism, form the central moving body of Christendom. The book read in the home has been added to the play enacted on the stage; has, in large measure, taken its place. It is an idle speculation to reflect whether Shakespeare if now living would choose the drama or the novel for his form; whichever he chose it is incontestible that his attitude toward human life would compel him to take into account a stage upon which kings and princes played but a feeble part in comparison with untitled men and women, whose passions, acts, thoughts, were about each other in their social and domestic relations far more than in political activity. In a word, the sphere of the plain man and woman has been enlarged out of all proportion to a similar enlargement of the sphere of the titular man and woman. To vary the emphasis of Shakespeare's words, —

> "All the world 's a stage
> And *all* the men and women merely players."

The absence of the democratic in Shakespeare is simply a witness to the limitations of the society which Shakespeare represented. It hints at one of those great silent changes in the constitution of humanity which will one day cause readers to see Shakespeare with different eyes from what men here and now look at him. The mere difference in costume and speech is easily corrected for us by diligent commentators, but a difference in political and social structure means a difference in habits of thought, and no short and sharp footnote will make this clear; only the mind trained to imaginative activity and possessed of historical knowledge will be able to understand and realize the distinction.

When, therefore, we seek to clarify our thought upon great ethical and social problems, and take down our Shakespeare, we find abundant illustration in almost every direction, and we cannot readily exhaust his capacity for illuminating our subjects; we might find a quotation from Shakespeare to stand as a motto at the head of every editorial in every daily newspaper to be published to-morrow in the United States. But all this illustration proceeds upon the agreement of our world with the world of Shakespeare's time; as we look more narrowly we are aware of certain tendencies on the part of this moving world of ours to drift away from Shakespeare's world. It is still within conversational distance; it will long be within hailing distance; it is safe to say that it never will be beyond communication, but the points of difference will grow more obvious, and as they thus are magnified, our consciousness of radical distinctions will grow more emphatic. We see all this on a large scale in the ever widening gulf between Englishmen and Americans. The Atlantic Ocean, which separates the two continents, has been contracting its space ever since the first Virginians rowed across its waters.

The inventions of men, the exactions of human intercourse, have reduced a three months' dreary voyage to a six days' trip in a movable hotel, and yet all this while a myriad forces have been at work on either side of the ocean moulding national consciousness, and producing those distinctions which are hard to express but perfectly patent. The manifestations of character in literature and art afford the clearest indications of this national distinction, and although London and Boston can almost speak to each other through the telephone, the accent of Boston in literature is more sharply discriminated from the accent of London than it was a hundred years ago.

Of what vast moment, then, it is, that the world of England in its most genetic period should have been compressed into a globe of art which we may turn and turn, exposing one continent after another to view. The farther we recede from Shakespeare's time, the more possible it is to isolate the period, to see it as a whole, and thus to use it as a factor in thought, just as we use Greece. Shakespeare then will be to us as the measuring rod by which we shall estimate proportions.